# Come Here, Jesus

## Barbara Cawthorne Crafton

Church Publishing
NEW YORK

Church Publishing
19 East 34th Street
New York, NY 10016

www.churchpublishing.org

Cover art: Noli me tangere by Wanda Ozieranska © 2018
Cover design by Jennifer Kopec, 2Pug Design
Typeset by Denise Hoff

Library of Congress Cataloging-in-Publication Data

Names: Crafton, Barbara Cawthorne, author.
Title: Come here, Jesus / Barbara Cawthorne Crafton.
Description: New York : Church Publishing, 2018. | Includes
    bibliographical references.
Identifiers: LCCN 2018027199 (print) | LCCN 2018039650 (ebook) |
    ISBN 9781640651203 (ebook) | ISBN 9781640651197 (pbk.)
Subjects: LCSH: Jesus Christ--Person and offices. | Witness bearing
    (Christianity)
Classification: LCC BT203 (ebook) | LCC BT203 .C73 2018 (print) |
    DDC 232--dc23
LC record available at https://lccn.loc.gov/2018027199

Printed in the United States of America

# Contents

∽

My daughter, Anna Crafton Walker, saw Jesus rather often when she was tiny. I used to wonder if perhaps we all can see him when we're little and just learn to edit these experiences out of our memory as we grow up, so people won't think we're crazy.

But Anna saw him, and she's not crazy.

I saw him once. You might have seen him.

You may yet.

I guess we all will.

This book about Jesus is dedicated to Anna, my great Dude.

∽

"Whose baby that?"

Sethe did not answer.

"You don't even know. Come here, Jesus." Amy sighed and shook her head. "Hurt?"

"A touch."

Sethe raised up on her elbows. Lying on her back for so long had raised a ruckus between her shoulder blades. The fire in her feet and the fire on her back made her sweat.

"My back hurt me," she said.

"Your back? Gal, you a mess. Turn over here and let me see." In an effort so great it made her sick to her stomach, Sethe turned on her right side. Amy unfastened the back of her dress and said, "Come here, Jesus," when she saw.

—Toni Morrison, *Beloved*

# Come Here, Jesus

I don't suppose there is much of anything in this book about Jesus that will be news to anyone. I do love the Scriptures, but I am no biblical scholar—probably I could name you a dozen people just in my neighborhood who are smarter than I am about the Bible. And I don't know how many books about Jesus there are, but I know there are a lot. So the impetus for my writing it was not any sense of the world's need to learn more about Jesus from the likes of me.

On the other hand, we have to learn about Jesus from *somebody*. Somebody has to tell us. Jesus has been told to people by other people for better than twenty centuries. There are things you only have to hear once and you've got it—no matter how many times you analyze table salt, it's always going to be sodium chloride. Look them up in as many atlases as you like, but the Alps will always be in Europe, and they won't be any more in Europe in fifty years than they are today.

Jesus is different. Him, we have to tell and retell. We mostly experience him in each other: in our ways of telling and, more importantly, in our ways of showing who he is. It is this that has prompted me to write a book about Jesus, something I never expected to do. I was all set to begin a book about forgiveness, which I *do* think will contain some things that will be news to many people. But then this happened.

*You need to write a book about Jesus.*

This was not a voice I *heard*. Not with my ears—nothing that spooky. It was just a thought that popped into my head one night when I woke up at about three a.m. And don't think there was anything remarkable about my waking up at that hour, either—when you get to be my age, you're for sure up a few times every night, and you consider one during which you arose only once to have been a good night's sleep. Those brief waking moments in the dark of night have become interesting times of reflection for me, times when I can entertain a thought or two without having to go and do something about it. But this one had an air of urgency. And it refused to leave.

*You need to write a book about Jesus.*

Well, all right then.

There must be a reason why it refuses to leave. We've already established that the reason is not my superior knowledge of biblical criticism. That's not what I'm bringing to the Jesus potluck. So why me? What *do* I have to bring?

I suppose I could bring some stories. People first met Jesus through stories—the ones he told. It was his favorite way of teaching, and it is mine as well. And then they met him again through stories other people told about him. First, it was people who had known him when he walked the earth. We always wish we had been one of them, so we could have a sure and certain faith in Jesus—forgetting that just about everybody who knew him well hightailed it out of there during and after the events surrounding his death, afraid for their lives. I doubt if we would have done any better. Then it was people who knew those people, and then it was people who had heard about those people, who had read the stories those people told about him. Layer after layer of Jesus-memory laid themselves down on the table of human history. We clustered around it, looking at this and that. There was more and more to look at all the time.

The ongoing life of Jesus had to *dawn* on people. It had to creep into their experience, and mostly it did so slowly—St. Paul got a sudden conversion, knocked to the ground and blinded by it, but most everybody else came to it by degrees, the way we do. Somebody in a gathering says something about Jesus that intrigues you, and you listen a little more closely. Then it's time to go home. You don't think about it for a couple of weeks. Then you hear something about him again, and you remember what that lady said a couple of weeks ago. You think maybe you should read the Bible, as you've always said you wanted to do, so you get the one you got from your aunt as a confirmation present down off the shelf, unzip it—it closed with a zipper!— and turn to the Gospels. You know to do *that* much.

You figure you'll start with Matthew, since it's the first one. But you see a long string of names right at the beginning, and they remind you of that time you tried to read the

Bible straight through when you were ten years old—you got bogged down in all the *begats* in the book of Genesis and gave up. So you turn to Mark, the second gospel. You are gratified to see that it is also the shortest.

As it happens, the preacher talks about Mark in church on Sunday. This is somewhat remarkable, as you are by no means a regular there—you really only go when your parents come to the city to visit you. But he talks about how, in Mark 1:9–11, the baptism of Jesus is a little different from the one in Matthew 3:13–17. In Matthew, a voice from heaven says "*This* is my beloved son," as if he were being introduced to the onlookers, while in Mark the voice seems to speak only to Jesus: "*You* are my beloved son." As if, maybe, only Jesus heard it. So the preacher goes on to say that maybe this was the moment when Jesus became aware of who he was.

And you are shocked. Wait, Jesus didn't always *know*? You had always assumed he knew everything at birth, that the toddler Jesus already had it all figured out. You sit in the pew and wish you'd toughed it out in Matthew, gotten through all the names and gotten to the baptism of Jesus. You now don't remember which chapter he said it was in, but you'll find it. So you can see for yourself.

*Come here, Jesus.*

# CHAPTER 1

# Jesus the Son of God

We might be forgiven for thinking that "Jesus, Son of God" means that Jesus was God's biological offspring—so much ink has been spilled in defense of the idea. The whole folk-loric edifice of the Virgin Birth, for instance, grew and grew in response to the church's need for Jesus not to have come into the world in the normal way. Once the word "virgin" as applied to his mother had come to mean that she didn't have sexual intercourse either before or after conceiving Jesus, there was no turning back. Among the things this entailed were the following:

1. Jesus cannot have had any brothers or sisters. This was necessary if Mary's virginity was understood to be perpetual. But sisters and brothers are mentioned in Mark 6:3, in Matthew 13:55–56, and in Matthew 12:47

("*Your mother and your brothers are standing outside, wanting to speak to you.*") James is referred to several times as "the brother of the Lord." A cousin? A stepbrother, Joseph's child from a previous marriage? Or just an expression indicating the closeness of their relationship? If so, he is the only one of the twelve referred to in that way. And it is not James who is described in terms of his emotional closeness to Jesus (the disciple "whom Jesus loved" in John 13:23). And *that* disciple is not called Jesus's brother. What to do?

2. Mary must also have been born without sin. If sin is communicated through sexual intercourse, as ancient and medieval theologians at least since St. Augustine believed, what then? The doctrine of the Immaculate Conception, accepted informally for centuries but not promulgated by any pope until 1854, holds that Mary was sinless even though her parents conceived her in the usual way. It was the foreknown merits of her son that kept her pure. Just how that worked remains a mystery.

3. What about Joseph? He disappears from the biblical texts after the birth narratives, and Mary is solitary and in need of care at the time of the crucifixion (*Woman, behold your son.*[1]) Joseph is usually depicted in art as being much, much older than Mary—safely

---

1. John 19:26.

unable to consummate much of anything. And yet, the genealogy in the beginning of the gospel according to Matthew, which is intended to connect Jesus with the house of David, is that of Joseph, not that of Mary. Her parentage is not mentioned in Scripture at all—Joachim and Anna, her parents, are the invention of a later era. Another puzzle.

I suppose one of the things we can take away from puzzles such as these is a healthy caution about loading more onto these ancient texts than they can bear. They were written by people, copied and recopied by other people—all human beings, like ourselves. Each book arose from a community bound together by the manner in which its members came to know Christ, and the communities were not all alike. It is certainly true that they were unlike us in many ways, and it is also true that we are not all alike, either. They had goals for their readers: they wrote so that their readers might think about Jesus in a certain way. We can learn much from these Christians who left us so long ago, but it would be unwise for us to try to become them. Aping the ancient church is not our project. Our project is to discover what in our day will do for us what their thoughts and visions did for them.

But if that is the case, if the Scriptures and their content are so community-relative, why need we revere them? Why can they not remain harmlessly on the dust heap of history? Why, when I was ordained an Episcopal priest nearly forty years ago, was I required to swear that I believed "the Holy Scriptures of the Old and New Testaments to be the Word of God, and to contain all things necessary to salvation"? And why, almost forty years later, will this year's ordinands still be required to affirm the same thing?[2] Why?

Because they connect us with the person of Jesus, with people's memories of him and other people's memories of those memories. Because a little girl can hear the words of Scripture two thousand years after Jesus was born and still imagine that they apply to her.

You may know that there was a movement in the early church to dispense with the Hebrew Scriptures (what Christians until fairly recently widely called "the Old Testament"). The person most identified with this movement was one Marcion, who lived and wrote in the middle of the first century, but he was not alone in rejecting the Hebrew Scriptures. Jesus was what was important, Marcionites reasoned, and *he* isn't even in the Old Testament. Besides, much of what they read in the ancient Hebrew texts offended them—such superstition! So many contradictions in it, and so little in the way of philosophy, of logic—it all felt much too primitive, especially to Christian converts who had not grown up within the fold of Judaism.

But the Marcionites and their ilk did not prevail. The Hebrew Scriptures would stay, and Christians would just have to reckon with them. Moreover— however luminously self-evident the books that *would* become the Christian Scriptures

---

2. The Ordination of a Priest, Book of Common Prayer, 526.

must have seemed to those who wrote them, reckoning with *them* is no picnic for us twenty centuries later, either. They, too, emerged from a world very different from ours, and we don't understand *that* world perfectly, either. It was a long time ago. There are many modern-day Marcionites, I imagine, who would just as soon ignore the whole Bible. Find Jesus in our own experience.

But how would we do that? How would we know it was Jesus? How would we move from the profound experience of oneness we have in meditation of any kind, Christian or no, to engagement with the person of Christ?

Would we even want to?

Without the Scriptures–warts and all—as our guide, we would lose touch with him. We would forget him.

In time, we wouldn't even experience the loss of him as a loss. Our faith might still be called "Christian," but it would no longer have much to do with Jesus. This idea has held a certain attraction for theologians, from time to time, providing as it does a rationale for not dealing with the chasm of cultural difference that separates us from Jesus and his century. Theologians refer to this as "the scandal of the particular." Baldly stated, it goes something like this: *Jesus was a man of his time. He thought and behaved like one. We should not take anything he says or does as normative. This or that may have been important to Jesus, but it need not be to us. All that should matter to us is the Cosmic Christ, the second person of the Trinity, who is the means by which the universe exists and who connects us with the power of that existence.*

So, never mind. There need be no conversation with Jesus of Nazareth. What he said doesn't matter—it doesn't even matter if he really said it or not. Unlike all our other relationships, we are free in this one to ignore the aspects of him we don't like. We can prune Jesus to our specifications. Think of it as theological topiary, and get out your clippers.

But relationship needs to be harder than that. At the very least, Jesus deserves a good wrestle. So does every last one of his followers, those who walked the earth with him and those who came after. And our descendants? They will have to wrestle with us. They will have to struggle with the fact that we claimed to follow the one through whom the earth is created and then shrugged off the fact that we smothered it every day with our polluting greed. They will be as mystified at our ability to worship with a happy heart while a third of the world's children went to bed hungry every night as we are by churchgoing slave owners before the American Civil War. They will be confounded by the fact that some among us called themselves "pro-life" but enthusiastically supported the death penalty.

When we contend with Jesus the Son of God, we contend with all of them. We contend first with his redactors, those who first wrote down the texts we now revere. And then with the ones who followed—every age has found in Jesus what it needed to find. He has not been the same throughout the ages. Each one has recast him in its own image. For us to acknowledge that this is the case is not to discount the value of any of these images—there was a reason for the choices

each made about who he would be for them. We may disavow
their choices—and we must disavow some of them—but we
cannot disown those people. In particular, we cannot disown
the ones whose Jesus repels us: the slaveholders' Jesus, the
Nazis' Jesus, the homophobes' Jesus; they are not ours, but
those people are ours. If we disown them, we may miss the
opportunity to learn from their errors, and then we will be in
danger of making the same ones. How does a follower of St.
Francis become an agent of colonization in the New World?
How does a Christian theologian become an apologist for the
Third Reich? How does the obsessively homophobic Westboro
Baptist Church come to insist that our God is a god of hate
and not of love? How does a mother disown her own son,
allowing him to die of AIDS in a hospital far away without
ever visiting him, and think that in this she is doing her duty
as a Christian? I saw this during the AIDS crisis in the 1980s
and 1990s, and I saw it more than once. How does a young
gunman apologize to his victims before killing them, telling
them that, though they seem like really good people, he must
now shoot them all because they are black and he is white?
To what spiritual need do such beliefs minister? We need to
know. Like it or not, our memory of Jesus is forever mixed
with theirs. Everything comes from somewhere.

This exploration is not for sissies.

When we speak of Jesus as the Son of God, we do well to
remember that the phrase meant more in biblical times than
simply a filial relationship by blood. Certainly such a limited view of it is understandable in light of our sacred texts:

consider the kerfuffle in Luke and especially in Matthew about the virgin birth, the genealogical lists in Matthew of who begot whom. A person could be pardoned for thinking that the most important thing to know about Jesus was who his father wasn't.

But Jesus himself locates familial relationship in more than blood, and sometimes in opposition to it:

> Who is my mother? Who are my brothers? And pointing to his disciples, he said, "Here are my mother and my brothers! For whoever does the will of my Father in heaven is my brother and sister and mother."[3]

> Anyone who loves their father or mother more than me is not worthy of me; anyone who loves their son or daughter more than me is not worthy of me.[4]

To be a son is to subordinate one's own will to the will of the Father. To reproduce the spirit of one generation in the next. Moreover, in assertions like "I and the Father are one" and "the Father is in me and I am in the Father," Jesus claims identity with God, not just filial relationship.

Like my friend Bob, who believed that God took his son from him because he loved him more than he loved God, Christians who imagine they must smother their obligation

3. Matt. 12:48–49.
4. Matt. 10:37.

of compassion toward other human beings beneath a blanket of their supposed duty to God can find themselves tragically opposed to their own hearts. They might also find themselves enlisted in a very ugly army. One thinks of the Crusades, for instance, or of the Inquisition in the sixteenth and seventeenth centuries. Of the Salem witch trials. Certainly of the Holocaust. All of these shredded with murderous thoroughness the bonds of simple human empathy toward outsiders.

If we cannot look beneath Jesus's troubling words about the competition between obligation to God and obligation to family and see a critique of the tribalism that tempts and infects human communities, we will think that God is indifferent or even hostile to the bonds of our common humanity. We will miss something important. It turns out to be easier than many of us imagine to become monstrous.

# Get Behind Me!

*Get behind me, Satan! You are a stumbling block to me; for you are setting your mind not on divine things, but on human things.*

*Matthew 16:23*

Well, that's a bit strong. All Peter was trying to do was save his friend's life. Who among us would not have given someone we loved the same advice? *Jerusalem?!? Now?!? Are you crazy?!?*

Sometimes the people you love do foolish things for no good reason, and you will move heaven and earth to try and stop them. In the end, you may not be *able* to stop them, and you will have to watch them reap what they have sown. In the end, the best you can hope for may be that the whole experience has been an unforgettable lesson.

And sometimes, someone you love takes a terrible risk for something very important, fully aware of what might happen. Again, perhaps, you move heaven and earth, and again you may not be able to stop it. And so you must watch as actions you have warned against yield to their consequences.

This time, though, the watching is very different. This time, the one doing most of the learning is probably you. You learn how brave he is, something you may not have known before. And you learn—again—that even the most potent love does not empower you to control the actions of another, that the really important things in life are far too important to entrust to another's decision. Even yours.

You want life with your beloved to go on forever, but it will not. If you try to protect your world as it is, to the exclusion of all else, you will lose all the joy of it while you are doing so. And, in the end, you will lose your world anyway.

We cannot cling to safety. We cannot make our whole life about being safe. We cannot clutch it to our chests—if we do, we will not have our arms free to embrace the world for the little time we have to live in it and love its life. It will be over, and we will have missed it.

# CHAPTER 2

# Jesus Who Knew Everything

Did Jesus make mistakes? Were there things he didn't know? Among the things we carry with us from childhood are questions like this, questions we may have asked someone we trusted when we were little. I recall impaling the adults in my family upon them myself, as I tried to make sense of my inherited faith and make it my own. How could all this be? How could there be a God who made mistakes? Everybody knows that God doesn't make mistakes. On the other hand, how could there be a human being who never made any? That's not human. Yet those seemed the only available options from which I might form a usable Christology, and they just didn't go together.

Truly God and truly human, that was Jesus. That much I knew. But I wanted to know how both were true. As I puzzled, which I did off and on throughout my growing up, I reinvented several of the major heresies.

Jesus was God, period. He only looked and acted like a human being. His suffering was not real. This was Docetism, which I invented sometime in the mid–1950s but which was actually condemned at the Council of Nicea in 325 CE.

Jesus was the Son of God, but was not himself God. He was created by God, a masterpiece. This was Arianism. I invented it, too, a little after my Docetic period. Actually, I commuted between the two heresies through most of my teenage years.

I was also an Appolinarianist at times: Jesus's body was human, but his mind was divine. I still know lots of Appolinarianists. You probably know a fair number yourself.

I was also a latter-day Adoptionist, especially as a teenager. Adoptionists believed that Jesus was born in the normal way and adopted by God at his baptism in the Jordan River. His life and death were chosen by God, but Jesus himself was a normal human being. Lots of people still are Adoptionists.

Jesus wasn't God at all. He wasn't even the Son of God. He was just a fine human being. This heresy leaps over the whole vexing problem of who and what Jesus was, and is, if the truth were told, held by most people today, including some of the people I love best. It doesn't really have a name.

But I wanted, and *continue* to want, something more than this about Jesus. I was not, and *am* not, willing to leave the Son of God part behind, though I am content for the term to designate something other than the miraculous overturning of reproductive biology—as far as I'm concerned, Mary need not have been a perpetual virgin in order for Jesus to be the Son of God. We know, for instance, that Jesus was often referred to as the "Son of David." The title was accorded him so often that Matthew was at pains to give us that long genealogy for Jesus at the beginning of his account, designed not only to trace Jesus's lineage to David through Joseph, but to spell it out numerically, relying on the mystical practice of *gematria*, a numerological approach to the words of Scripture which was full of meaning to Matthew, though it is of interest mostly to scholars today.[1] Here it is:

Each letter of the Hebrew alphabet has a corresponding number, and the numbers have mystical significance—six days of creation, a seventh day of rest, twelve tribes of Israel.

The numbers corresponding to the three consonants in David's name add up to fourteen.

Each of the three sets of forebears in Matthew's genealogy contains fourteen generations.

See?

No, that might not make modern hearts beat faster (though the *content* of the lists does make mine flutter a bit—the presence of Ruth, Rahab, Tamar, and Bathsheba among them).[2] But it did touch *their* hearts, the ancient people who heard these lists read, whose teachers explained it to them. It would have thrilled them: *See, Jesus really does go all the way back*

---

1. For some more about *gematria*, see Gutman G. Locks, *The Spice of Torah: Gematria* (New York: Judaica Press, 2012).

2. The three-part genealogy of Jesus, found in Matthew 1, includes some resourceful women, all of whom employ their sexuality to turn the tables on powerful men. For Rahab the harlot, see Joshua 2:1, 3; 6:17–25. For Tamar, see Genesis 38. Ruth (with her mother-in-law Naomi) is so resourceful that an entire book is devoted to her. Bathsheba ("the wife of Uriah the Hittite") is also there—she is famous, too, though not for her resourcefulness. Her story is in the eleventh chapter of 2 Samuel.

*to David, in orderly clumps of fourteen! The numbers don't lie, they would have said to themselves. They show that God has a plan, and everything points toward it, if you just know how to look for it! History may seem chaotic while we are living it, but it is really a beautiful and stately dance.* So a biological connection to the line of David mattered to the first Christians, for whom making a case for Jesus as the eagerly awaited Messiah was important. They were Jews, hoping to convince other Jews. History mattered. Prophecy mattered. David mattered. Jesus was the fulfilment of all of it.

That the world has an intrinsic orderliness matters deeply to people for whom much in life is beyond their control, as was true of ancient people. The mechanics of maintaining life were less dependable then than they are now. Disease, pestilence, cataclysmic weather events—we have all these things too, of course, but we have more tools with which to face them than they did. While it is certainly true that all our tools fail us in the end, we can extend our run much longer than they could. When they thought of a man who was also God, then, one of the ways in which they would have expected that to manifest itself would be that the secrets of a universe unmanageable to us would not be secrets to him. Necessarily, he would know the future. He would read minds. He would control nature. We would never see him taken aback, as we are so often taken aback.

> Then Jesus looked up and said, "Father, I thank you that you have heard me. I knew that you always hear me, but I said this for the benefit of

the people standing here, that they may believe that you sent me."[3]

For he knew who was going to betray him, and that was why he said not everyone was clean.[4]

The woman answered him, "I have no husband." Jesus said to her, "You are right in saying, 'I have no husband'; for you have had five husbands, and the one you have now is not your husband. What you have said is true!" The woman said to him, "Sir, I see that you are a prophet."[5]

When Jesus saw Nathanael coming towards him, he said of him, "Here is truly an Israelite in whom there is no deceit!" Nathanael asked him, "Where did you come to know me?" Jesus answered, "I saw you under the fig tree before Philip called you." Nathanael replied, "Rabbi, you are the Son of God! You are the King of Israel!" Jesus answered, "Do you believe because I told you that I saw you under the fig tree? You will see greater things than these." And he said to him, "Very truly, I tell you, you will see heaven opened and the angels of God ascending and descending upon the Son of Man."[6]

3. John 11:41–42.
4. John 13:11.
5. John 4:17–19.
6. John 1:47–51.

He said to him the third time, "Simon, son of John, do you love me?" Peter felt hurt because he said to him the third time, "Do you love me?" And he said to him, "Lord, you know everything; you know that I love you." Jesus said to him, "Feed my sheep. Very truly, I tell you, when you were younger, you used to fasten your own belt and to go wherever you wished. But when you grow old, you will stretch out your hands, and someone else will fasten a belt around you and take you where you do not wish to go." (He said this to indicate the kind of death by which he would glorify God.) After this he said to him, "Follow me."[7]

*Lord, you know everything.* He knew everything.

Notice that all these examples are from the Gospel of John. Jesus strides through John's Gospel like Paul Bunyan—never surprised, never in doubt, possessed of knowledge no one else has. John's version of Jesus is easily the most clairvoyant Jesus in all the Gospels—and yet it is only in John that we see Jesus weep, approaching the tomb of his friend Lazarus. Our commitment to the Jesus Who Knew Everything gives us pause when we read of his tears.

When Jesus saw her weeping, and the Jews who came with her also weeping, he was greatly disturbed in spirit and deeply moved. He said,

---

7. John 21:17–19.

"Where have you laid him?" They said to him, "Lord, come and see." Jesus began to weep. So the Jews said, "See how he loved him!"[8]

Jesus was *disturbed*? Wait—what happened to the Jesus who sails with calm confidence above everyone else's angst? And, of all places for us to be confronted with this weeping Jesus, in the Gospel of John?!? Jesus *wept*?

We are out of control when we cry. Our faces crumple unrecognizably. I remember weeping once when I was leaving my four-year-old grandson after a visit: I frightened him, because I didn't look like myself. "I don't like that face," he said, shrinking back against his mother, and we both hastened to reassure him. *"It's okay. Mamo was just sad. She's all right now."*

Sad about Lazarus. Angry at the moneychangers in the temple—*You have made it a den of thieves!*[9] Impatient at the people's lack of understanding—*An evil generation asks for a sign.* Lonely and hurt—*Then he came to the disciples and found them sleeping; and he said to Peter, "So, could you not stay awake with me one hour?"* Frightened in the garden of Gethsemane—*Let this cup pass from me!* We have seen Jesus in all of these states in the Gospels, and in none of them does he look like Jesus Who Knew Everything. He looks like a human being, subject to the same emotions we experience, not like someone who already knows all will be well. He is in the struggle, and he is vulnerable to it. This is what it means to be truly human.

---

8. John 11:33–36.
9. Matt. 21:13; Mark 11:17; Luke 19:46; John 2:14–16.

Then what does it mean to be truly God? Whatever else he is, Jesus cannot be the detached God of the philosophers, the unmoved mover standing outside of human experience. Nor can this God be the monstrous baptizer of his own impulses: God cannot be like the emperor gods of Rome. This God, in short, is not primarily characterized by absolute autonomy, but by indelible union with the finitude of the created order of which we are a part. There is no secret trap door through which to exit this union, no shortcut. Jesus does not beat the system.

> Those who passed by derided him, shaking their heads and saying, "You who would destroy the temple and build it in three days, save yourself! If you are the Son of God, come down from the cross."[10]

But he does not. He can't—he is nailed there. In embracing our nature he has also embraced our prison. He must pass through what we must pass through, and he is doing it before our eyes.

His embrace of our nature must include our limited vision, or it is an incomplete embrace and a charade. Far from being offensive, the idea that Jesus was sometimes mistaken is essential to a mature view of the Incarnation. In order to be one of us, he had to be wrong sometimes. He had to learn the way we learn, which is primarily by making mistakes and correcting them. Our failures are an important part of us—we

---

10. Matt. 27:39–40.

would not know what we know without acknowledging them. You need not look further than the next person you encounter who cannot admit to ever having been wrong—his claim does not ring true. If to err is indeed human, then not to err is inhuman. In the Incarnation, the one through whom the universe is created must enter into our error as well as embody our virtues, or there is an important aspect of being human he will not know. Ultimate power must live within the limits of great weakness.

And no, we don't know how that can be. Ponder it for the rest of your life and you still will not know. But the fact that we are unable to reconcile Christ's two natures does not mean that Christ cannot have two natures. It just means that we lack the ability either to understand or to explain them.

On the other hand, we know some things *he* did not know. For instance, Jesus believed in demons as malevolent personalities. He believed that they caused illnesses. Everyone believed this, in his day. A number of his healing miracles involved the exorcism of such demons. We, on the other hand, do not believe that illness is demonic in origin. We look to other causes—germs, of whose existence Jesus was unaware, or a malfunction of the immune system in which our bodies turn against themselves. Insofar as is possible, we marshal our scientific resources to combat disease, and sometimes we succeed. Sometimes we do not. And sometimes, a person with a disease we know to be fatal recovers, for reasons we cannot explain. At such times, we shake our heads and declare it a mystery— come to think of it, perhaps *mystery* would be a better word to use than *miracle* in *all* such cases. *My terminal patient didn't die*, an old physician recalls. *She got better and lived. I didn't know how. This was fifty years ago, and I still don't know.*

So who is right? Who is real? Is it Jesus, who heals by casting out demons? Is it the sachem, who heals with herbs, or the acupuncturist, who inserts tiny needles under your skin? Your doctor, who heals with an antibiotic? Is it your neurosurgeon, who excises your brain tumor with a gamma knife? Each takes a different path. None of them succeed every time—we read of Jesus being unable to perform many miracles in his home town:

> "Is not this the carpenter's son? Is not his mother called Mary? And are not his brothers James and Joseph and Simon and Judas? And are not all his sisters with us? Where then did this man get all this?" And they took offence at him. But Jesus said to them, "Prophets are not without honor except in their own country and in their own house." And he did not do many deeds of power there, because of their unbelief.[11]

What if the power of Jesus is something other than the magical power we so often attribute to him? What if his divinity lies instead in the fact of his identity and complete alignment with the power of the universe, that driving energetic force that pushed back nothingness and brought *being* into being? What

---

11. Matt. 13:55–58.

if *that* is the way in which his mysteries happen—if, rather than acting *upon* the sick, he acts in concert with them, with their God-given tendency toward life and away from death? What if each miracle is a recapitulation of the original something-out-of-nothing miracle of existence itself? What if each miracle proclaims not itself, but the prior mystery of relatedness which has its root in the original oneness that birthed a whole diverse universe? Then we might look in a different light at Jesus's shyness about proclaiming the miracles:

> Jesus answered them, "Very truly, I tell you, you are looking for me, not because you saw signs, but because you ate your fill of the loaves. Do not work for the food that perishes, but for the food that endures for eternal life, which the Son of Man will give you. For it is on him that God the Father has set his seal."[12]

Heal the sick, give voice to the mute, sight to the blind, give music to the ears of those who cannot hear—eventually all of them will die of something. None of them—not the woman healed of her hemorrhage, not the blind man who received his sight, not the man who was delivered of the many demons, not Jairus's little daughter raised from the dead—none of them are alive today. All went on with their lives and then on into death. The healing of our mortal ills may be spectacular, but it is also temporary. All of our clocks run down.

---

12. John 6:26–27. Here, Jesus refers to the miraculous feeding of the five thousand.

Jesus's experience of this must be genuine, as his sorrow over his friend's death must be genuine, or he is not truly one of us. His tears must be real. He must know the same loss of control we know when we weep. To deny this is to deny who Jesus is.

An intellectual exercise? Theological sparring for those who enjoy that sort of thing? The question of Jesus's foreknowledge of events and outcomes is more than that for us. For centuries, we have aspired to appropriate to ourselves the view we thought Jesus had of human history. We have counseled one another to focus on heaven as a means of surviving the pain we experience here on earth. We have tried and failed repeatedly not to be disheartened when we couldn't see exactly how everything would turn out right in the end. We attributed all our events to God's "plan," seeing God as the cosmic mapper of our fortunes. This was a plan to which we were not privy, but it was most certainly a plan. God may not play dice with the universe, as Albert Einstein once said, but we were pretty sure he *did* play chess with it. God must move us around strategically, we thought, from square to square to square.

We thought about God's plan because we thought that God shared the linearity of our experience. It appears to us that our lives unfold along a line, one thing after another. Almost always, our linear way of thinking about our experience of life here under the sun serves us well. But lately, we have had glimpses of life that is not under the sun. Our eyes have journeyed outside its neighborhood, peering into stunning images of other worlds, other solar systems, other galaxies. We have run the numbers and concluded that there could be—in fact, there must be—other whole universes, other dimensions, other ways of being of which we have no experience beyond the theoretical necessity of their existence. Now we must think of a more complex model of God's time, understanding as we now do that even our experience of time is much more multidimensional than we ever dreamed it was.

And what might all this have to do with our omniscient Jesus? The Jesus Who Knew Everything, who knew in 24 CE that I would make onion soup for supper on a chilly February evening a little more than two thousand years later? Who planned the menu on my behalf, directing my slicing of the onions, the tearing of my eyes, my stirring of the pot as the white slices turned golden and then a lovely dark brown? Who foreknew my eleventh-hour discovery that we were out of Gruyère, and guided me to choose another cheese from the icebox for the gratin, rather than dropping everything and running out to the store? Who then encouraged me to chop up some garlic and add it to the mix, since I was already departing from French culinary tradition by substituting an alien cheese?

Our linear model of God cannot imagine Jesus's presence in the events of our lives in any other manner than that of causation. If Jesus is in my life, we reason, he must be there as author of every detail of it. But the kingdom of heaven does not run on our clocks, which keep accurate time only here. Our clocks are parenthetical at best in God's experience: not absent from it (for nothing is absent from it) but not governing it. Causation depends on the before-and-after linearity of the model of time we have created for ourselves, but that is not an ultimate reality. If there is no real *before* to anything, it doesn't matter who caused it. In the eternal present of God, everything just *is*. What is eternally important is not *why* something happens, but *that* it happens. The crystalline structure of history—not just our world's history, but the history of the universe—hangs together in the simultaneity of God's beholding. The drama of it may unfold for us, scene by scene, but the whole of it is present to God.

So the divine plan, upon which we lean when we struggle to explain the inexplicable and defend the indefensible, depends for its existence on something which ultimately does not exist. Time rules us here, but in the domain of God there can be no time, not in the sense of duration. Of elapsing. Of changing from one state to another. God does not need things to change from one state to another, since everything—in every state it ever finds itself—exists concurrently in the beholding of One who can behold it thus, as we cannot.

Ancient Christian theologians, as well as pagan philosophers both before them and contemporary with them, embraced the idea of God's changelessness. It is one of our inherited basic beliefs: God does not change, does not experience the loss that change brings to humankind. We read the Hebrew Scriptures and see Yahweh changing his mind now and then, and it embarrasses us a little—God seems too human.[13] *Wait, that can't be right, we mutter to ourselves. God can't change his plan, can he?*

---

13. God changes his mind in these and other passages from the Hebrew scriptures: Exod. 33:17, 1 Sam. 15:11, 2 Sam. 24:16, 1 Chron. 21:15, Jon. 3:10, Ps. 106:45, Jer. 26:19.

But this is only a difficulty if God plans the way we plan, before things happen. The simultaneity of the divine beholding of all that *is* makes such a planning mode unnecessary. God lives around and alongside our linearity, includes our befores and our afters, but is not limited or determined by them, as we experience ourselves to be.

Letting go of the divine plan is disconcerting for us. We want there to be a plan. We need one. I know a man whose son—his only child—died in the healthy flower of his young adulthood, felled by a virus that came from nowhere and killed him within a couple of days. A conservative Catholic, Bob believes that this happened because he loved his son more than he loved God. You're not supposed to do that.

My blood ran cold when he first told me this. As delicately as I could, I proffered other ways in which he might think of his tragedy, but Bob stuck with that one. *God did this to me.* For Bob, this terrible reason was better than no reason. It was better to live with such a God than to live with so violent a shattering of his heart with no causal hook upon which to hang it.

*Come here, Jesus.*

Faced with a similar choice, Jesus is questioned about his healing of a man blind from birth. He invites those looking on, as well as the theological teachers of the day, to move beyond the anchor of causation as they consider this healing:

> As he walked along, he saw a man blind from birth. His disciples asked him, "Rabbi, who sinned, this man or his parents, that he was born blind?" Jesus answered, "Neither this man nor his

> parents sinned; he was born blind so that God's
> works might be revealed in him. As long as it is
> day, we must do the works of him who sent me.
> Night is coming, when no one can work. While
> I am in the world, I am the light of the world."
> When he had said this, he spat on the ground
> and made mud with the saliva and spread the
> mud on the man's eyes, saying to him, "Go, wash
> in the pool of Siloam" (which means Sent). Then
> he went and washed and came back able to see.[14]

Jesus resists an inquiry which would search the past for
meaning in the man's blindness. He is like Job. He refuses to
link the affliction to the simple calculus of cause and effect. The
writer widens the inquiry; it was the disciples questioning Jesus
first, and now the neighbors and bystanders want to know more.

> The neighbors and those who had seen him before
> as a beggar began to ask, "Is this not the man
> who used to sit and beg?" Some were saying, "It
> is he." Others were saying, "No, but it is someone
> like him." He kept saying, "I am the man." But
> they kept asking him, "Then how were your eyes
> opened?" He answered, "The man called Jesus
> made mud, spread it on my eyes, and said to me,
> 'Go to Siloam and wash.' Then I went and washed

---

14. John 9:1–7.

and received my sight." "Where is this man?" they asked him. "I do not know," he said.[15]

The Pharisees weigh in, adding a little confusion to the mix: Jesus is offending against the law by performing this healing on the Sabbath.[16]

> They brought to the Pharisees the man who had formerly been blind. Now it was a Sabbath day when Jesus made the mud and opened his eyes. Then the Pharisees also began to ask him how he had received his sight. He said to them, "He put mud on my eyes. Then I washed, and now I see." Some of the Pharisees said, "This man is not from God, for he does not observe the Sabbath." But others said, "How can a man who is a sinner perform such signs?" And they were divided. Then they turned again to the blind man, "What have you to say about him? It was your eyes he opened." The man replied, "He is a prophet."[17]

Perhaps there's been some mistake. Maybe it wasn't a miracle at all. Let's find out.

> The Jews did not believe that he had been blind and had received his sight until they called the parents

---

15. John 9:8–12.

16. It's my view that people who first heard this line must have found it very funny—a miracle has happened, and the righteous people all but ignore it, to focus instead on the niceties of Sabbath observance.

17. John 9:13–17.

of the man who had received his sight and asked them, "Is this your son, who you say was born blind? How then does he now see?" His parents answered, "We know that this is our son, and that he was born blind; but we do not know how it is that now he sees, nor do we know who opened his eyes. Ask him; he is of age. He will speak for himself."[18]

More interrogation by the Pharisees. By now it is clear that they don't *want* to believe in this miracle. They view it as what today might be called "fake news."

So for the second time they called the man who had been blind, and they said to him, "Give glory to God! We know that this man is a sinner." He answered, "I do not know whether he is a sinner. One thing I do know, that though I was blind, now I see." They said to him, "What did he do to you? How did he open your eyes?" He answered them, "I have told you already, and you would not listen. Why do you want to hear it again? Do you also want to become his disciples?" Then they reviled him, saying, "You are his disciple, but we are disciples of Moses. We know that God has spoken to Moses, but as for this man, we do not know where he comes from." The man answered, "Now that is remarkable! You don't know where he comes from,

---

18. John 9:18–21.

yet he opened my eyes. We know that God does not listen to sinners. He listens to the godly person who does his will. Nobody has ever heard of opening the eyes of a man born blind. If this man were not from God, he could do nothing." They answered him, "You were born entirely in sins, and are you trying to teach us?" And they drove him out.[19]

Like my bereaved friend Bob, the Pharisees can't bring themselves to leave their belief in a particular kind of causality behind. They are prepared to ignore hard evidence in order to maintain it. We leave them there.

Jesus heard that they had thrown him out, and when he found him, he said, "Do you believe in the Son of Man?" "Who is he, sir?" the man asked. "Tell me so that I may believe in him." Jesus said, "You have now seen him; in fact, he is the one speaking with you." Then the man said, "Lord, I believe," and he worshiped him. Jesus said, "For judgment I have come into this world, so that the blind will see and those who see will become blind." Some Pharisees who were with him heard him say this and asked, "What? Are we blind too?" Jesus said, "If you were blind, you would not be guilty of sin; but now that you claim you can see, your guilt remains."[20]

19. John 9:24–34.
20. John 9:35–41.

In this healing and the exchanges with others about it, Jesus seems uninterested in the causes of affliction. He doesn't want to talk about the man's past, or the past of his parents. It is true that in Scripture Jesus often speaks from out of our linearity. Of course he does—he is a human being, and is as subject to it as we are. But this Jesus is also the Jesus who was raised from the dead, opening the way into the divine and clock-less eternity. It is *this* bondage, our bondage to time, which he breaks down in the Resurrection. We mistake his victory for the destruction of earthly death itself, setting ourselves up for an irrational belief in our own immortality, as if being Christian somehow meant that we would not die. We know that some in the early church did think that about themselves, overlooking—as we sometimes do—the fact that Jesus himself died, as has everyone who has ever followed him. Whatever else it is, the Resurrection is not an end run around the death of our mortal body. It is participation in the fact that everything about us exists within the complicated origami of time and space, of which our linear experience of time and space is only a part.

Thus, the things that Jesus knows are not the same things a clairvoyant in a circus sideshow might know, even if we do sometimes read of him speaking and behaving as if it were, especially in the Gospel of John. The most important thing about Jesus is not that he runs our lives and directs our histories: it is that he invites us to transcend them, including everything that is in the much larger basket of everything that might be.

But let's not be too hard on the imaginings of our future we entertain in our more concrete moments. When someone dies and we say things like "We'll meet again" or "Now she's with her husband again, after all these years alone," we are not mistaken about that. Human life is not inferior to the life of the spirit: it is *part* of it. All of our moments *are* contained within the timeless present of God, including those human moments of fellowship we miss so much when they are taken from us. The fact of my loss and subsequent loneliness is part of that domain, along with the entire lifetime of love we enjoyed together before that loss occurred. Not a moment of it is lost to the reality of God. And so we *are* both there, meeting again and meeting for the first time, kissing for the first time and kissing goodnight for the last time, closing our eyes in death and opening them again to a new life. The past, the present, and the future are all one moment. They have always been one moment.

Think of it: the entire history of the universe. One moment.

> "I am the Alpha and the Omega," says the Lord God, who is and who was and who is to come, the Almighty.[21]

> Grace to you and peace from him who is and who was and who is to come, and from the seven spirits who are before his throne, and from Jesus Christ, the faithful witness, the firstborn of the dead, and the ruler of the kings of the earth.[22]

---

21. Rev. 1:8.
22. Rev. 1:4–5.

And the one who was seated on the throne said, "See, I am making all things new." Also he said, "Write this, for these words are trustworthy and true." Then he said to me, "It is done! I am the Alpha and the Omega, the beginning and the end.[23]

"Very truly I tell you," Jesus answered, "before Abraham was born, I am!"[24]

Thus says the Lord, the King of Israel, and his Redeemer, the Lord of hosts:

> I am the first and I am the last; besides me there is no god.[25]

Listen to me, O Jacob, and Israel, whom I called: I am He; I am the first, and I am the last.[26]

But Moses said to God, "If I come to the Israelites and say to them, 'The God of your ancestors has sent me to you,' and they ask me, 'What is his name?' what shall I say to them?" God said to Moses, "I AM WHO I AM." He said further, "Thus you shall say to the Israelites, 'I AM has sent me to you.'" God also said to Moses, "Thus you shall say to the Israelites, 'The Lord, the God of your ancestors, the God of

---

23. Rev. 21:5–6.
24. John 8:58.
25. Isa. 44:6.
26. Isa. 48:12.

Abraham, the God of Isaac, and the God of Jacob,
has sent me to you': This is my name forever, and
this my title for all generations."[27]

He is the Alpha AND the Omega. He is the I AM Moses
met in the burning bush, that existence in whom everything
exists. When we die, bringing our current way of being alive
to an end, we will know Christ with more immediacy than we
are equipped to know now, because we will be part of Christ.
This will be as much a matter of seeing as of anything else,
which makes John's story of Jesus and the man born blind
doubly eloquent. It is the wall that now seems to separate us
from God that disappears. Neither Moses nor Jesus will have
to teach us anything, because our knowledge will be God's
knowledge, our will God's will, God's law "written on our
hearts." This is true already, in fact, though ordinarily we do
not perceive it, and certainly we seldom show it in the slice of
partial reality we inhabit. True already, and has always been
true. We and everything that is: we are one thing.

---

27. Exod. 3:13–15.

# CHAPTER 3

# Jesus the Victim

Who was the guilty?
  Who brought this upon Thee?
Alas, my treason, Jesus, hath undone Thee.
'Twas I, Lord, Jesus, I it was denied Thee!
I crucified Thee.

> Johann Heermann, 1630,
> trans. Robert Bridges, 1899

For the first few hundred years, Christian art didn't focus on the crucifixion. Artists emphasized other things—Christ as a king. Christ who looked steadily back at you from his heavenly abode of gold mosaic, with piercing dark eyes that saw everything. Christ baptized by John, the two of them standing in water—in some depictions, fish swim back and forth around their legs. The risen Christ, strong and mighty, hauling the dead out of Hell and back up into the light. Christ at the Last Supper. Christ amid the apostles. Christ healing people of diseases. Christ casting out demons. Christ raising Lazarus from the dead.

But you won't see many images from the early centuries of Jesus himself dying. Crucifixes came later. Once they began to appear, though, there was no stopping them. The crucified Christ was everywhere: looking down at his sorrowing mother and his best friend, at clusters of other saints. Sometimes Christ the king and Christ the victim were joined in the same stately image, richly robed, his nimbus a crown, the folds of his garment hanging neatly, without a wrinkle, no sign of suffering in his impassive face. Often the garment was a priest's chasuble. We were still skittish, in those days, about the notion that Jesus really could suffer and die as we do. Died, perhaps, but surely not the way we die? Surely his dignity remained intact to the end. For a long time, artists shrank from the ugly reality of what a death like his must have been like.

Until they didn't. Then his pain was everywhere, too, his pain and his blood. Now Jesus sagged upon the cruel instrument of his torture. Now we saw blood and bruises, now a dead face, a swollen mouth gaping open, eyes sunken into the hollows of their sockets, never to open again. Now nothing about him was too ugly to show.

> He had no beauty or majesty to attract us to him, nothing in his appearance that we should desire him. He was despised and rejected by humankind, a man of suffering, and familiar with pain. Like one from whom people hide their faces he was despised, and we held him in low esteem.[1]

---

1. Isa. 53:2–3.

The early Christians were made uncomfortable by the same thing that sparked the derision of their pagan neighbors: *Your faith makes no sense! God can't suffer—gods are greater than we are.* The one through whom creation comes to be cannot himself be limited by that which limits us. A god might *pretend* to be mortal—like Zeus, say, who sometimes disguised himself as a mortal so he could seduce a mortal woman (and on one memorable occasion transformed himself into a swan for the same purpose). Or Hermes, who also had incognito conquests among mortal women. But these were mere charades of the gods. None of them affected their divine nature.

Take a look at this second century contribution to the history of satirical graffiti, found in Rome in the mid-nineteenth century during the excavation of a building that had been used as a boarding house for the imperial pages. It reads "Alexamenos worships his God."

It is easy to imagine a teenager scratching this crude drawing into the plaster of his dormitory wall, to torment a Christian classmate. The young artist's name is lost to us, but poor Alexamenos lives on, a permanent footnote to the history of adolescent bullying.[2]

Crucifixion would remain a feature of life in the Roman empire until Constantine abolished it in the fourth century. That it was agonizing goes without saying, but equally important in its administration was the humiliation of the crucified. The victims were naked throughout the whole of their ordeal.

---

2. Note that the crucified god has the head of a donkey: there were rumors in the early decades of the common era that Christians worshipped donkeys. I can't imagine why.

The loincloth we see draped tastefully across Jesus's hips in artists' depictions of the event is a concession to the decorum of subsequent ages: Jesus must certainly have been crucified in the nude. This would have been doubly shameful in a city like Jerusalem, whose Jewish residents abhorred public nudity. Crucifixion was a public event, valuable for its deterrent effect on the populace. That Joseph of Arimathea was granted permission to remove Jesus's body and give it a decent burial was unusual—typically, the rotting bodies of those executed in this way hung right where they were until they had been picked clean by vultures.

> Faithful Cross! above all other, one and only
>     noble Tree!
> None in foliage, none in blossom, none in fruit
>     thy peers may be;
> Sweetest wood and sweetest iron!
> Sweetest Weight is hung on thee!
>
> Venantius Fortunatus, 570

Sweet? The cross? About as sweet as a hangman's noose or an electric chair. But I can understand the impulse, I suppose. Early Christians may have wished to avoid the cross as much as they could, but it was a fact. Paul, who emerged as the foremost spokesperson of the new faith, insisted on it.

> For Jews demand signs and Greeks desire wisdom,
> but we proclaim Christ crucified, a stumbling-block
> to Jews and foolishness to Gentiles, but to those
> who are the called, both Jews and Greeks, Christ

the power of God and the wisdom of God. For
God's foolishness is wiser than human wisdom, and
God's weakness is stronger than human strength.[3]

We can have confidence that the death of Jesus on the
cross is authentic precisely because it is not something an
ancient Christian apologist with any sense would want to
invent. It was a strike against the new faith, not an argument
for it. This argument about a text, by the way, is known as
"the criterion of embarrassment"! Almost any other death
for Jesus would have been preferable to this one—a noble
suicide, like that of Socrates, perhaps. Or death at the hands
of an assassin, like Julius Caesar. Or even a beheading, like
the death of John the Baptist: it was violent, but it was quick.
That crucifixion was the death everyone who wrote about
it agreed had happened to Jesus would have been a repel-
lent idea to many people. Yet there it was: Jesus's passion
and death on the cross was the first story about Jesus to be
written and circulated. People molded its events into stories
before they did so with anything else, before the miracles
or the ethical teachings became recognizable paragraphs,
repeated from writer to writer. Even before they shaped the
resurrection narratives. Nobody would have *wanted* the crucifixion to be true. It's hard to imagine a reason other than
its authenticity to insist upon it as they did.

And so the artists and writers, the hymnists and the poets
down the centuries took a hideous fact and called it sweet.

---

3. 1 Cor. 1:22–25.

And in calling it sweet, they made it sweet, for Christian audiences. For another approach to the cross, interview a friend or two from another faith. Ask them how *they* view images of the crucifixion.

Why did we sweeten the cross? Why do we love Jesus the victim, savoring his every wound? We journey back to the beginning of our faith for a clue. It is one word.

The word is *for.*

> It is rare indeed for anyone to die **for** a righteous man, though **for** a good man someone might possibly dare to die. But God proves His love for us in this: While we were still sinners, Christ died **for** us. Therefore, since we have now been justified by His blood, how much more shall we be saved from wrath through Him![4]

> He was delivered over to death **for** our trespasses and was raised to life for our justification.[5]

> For at just the right time, while we were still powerless, Christ died **for** the ungodly.[6]

> He who did not spare His own Son but gave Him up **for** us all, how will He not also, along with Him, freely give us all things.[7]

---

4. Rom. 5:7–9.
5. Rom. 4:25.
6. Rom. 5:6.
7. Rom. 8:32.

> I have been crucified with Christ, and I no longer
> live, but Christ lives in me. The life I live in the
> body, I live by faith in the Son of God, who loved
> me and gave Himself up **for** me.[8]

> And walk in love, just as Christ loved us and gave
> Himself up **for** us as a fragrant sacrificial offering
> to God.[9]

> Greater love has no one than this, that he lay down
> his life **for** his friends.[10]

Jesus doesn't just die. He dies *for* us.

Christians did not invent the idea of substitutionary
atonement. It was ancient long before we came along. In
Leviticus 16, we encounter the idea of the scapegoat: two
goats are brought, one to be sacrificed and the other to be
left alive. The priest lays his hands on the second goat and
confesses all the sins of the people. Then it is driven out to
the wilderness.

> He shall take from the congregation of the people
> of Israel two male goats for a sin offering. . . . He
> shall take the two goats and set them before the
> Lord at the entrance of the tent of meeting; and
> Aaron shall cast lots on the two goats, one lot for

---

8. Gal. 2:20.

9. Eph. 5:2.

10. John 15:13.

the Lord and the other lot for Azazel.[11] Aaron shall present the goat on which the lot fell for the LORD, and offer it as a sin offering; but the goat on which the lot fell for Azazel shall be presented alive before the LORD to make atonement over it, that it may be sent away into the wilderness to Azazel. . . . Then Aaron shall lay both his hands on the head of the live goat, and confess over it all the iniquities of the people of Israel, and all their transgressions, all their sins, putting them on the head of the goat, and sending it away into the wilderness by means of someone designated for the task. The goat shall bear on itself all their iniquities to a barren region; and the goat shall be set free in the wilderness. [12]

Later, some of the rabbinical writers had it that the unhappy animal was thrown off a cliff, not just run out of the city and set free, lest it return and bring calamity with it. I bring this up only because it sheds an interesting light on a moment Luke recounts, when Jesus returned to his home town, preached briefly, and was taken to a cliff from which it was the crowd's intention to throw him.

---

11. Azazel was the name of a fallen angel, and may also be a term for the *condition* of having fallen away from God.

12. Lev. 16:5–22.

> They got up, drove him out of the town, and led
> him to the brow of the hill on which their town was
> built, so that they might hurl him off the cliff.[13]

No, we did not invent substitutionary atonement. The tradition of animal sacrifice is built on it. So is the requirement of circumcision—the symbolic sacrifice of a tiny portion of a life, rather than the whole of it. Embedded in our tradition—and still tucked among the stories, there for us to see if we can bear to see it—is the certainty that human sacrifice, especially the sacrifice of children, was a part of religious life in ancient Israel. The temple sacrifices of animals with which Jesus was familiar represent a tempering of this savage history. God was entitled to the blood of the innocent, but we might be able to satisfy him with the sacrifice of a lesser being. A lamb. A calf. A pair of doves.

Not a child.

Well, not any more.

We know that Israel's neighbors worshiped gods who demanded the sacrifice of children. Kronos, Saturn, some of the Baals—Moloch was the principal one mentioned in the Hebrew Scriptures. Firstborn children were ritually burned alive—apparently in a hollow bronze image of the god, which was also an incinerator. In the northern African city of Carthage, parents who could afford it sometimes conscripted other people's children to take the place of their own children in the ritual. Those children's impoverished parents were

---

13. Luke 4:29.

compensated for their loss, but had to watch the sacrifice—and would forfeit the money they had been promised if they protested or cried out. The playing of musical instruments, singing, and the loud banging of drums served to drown out the screams of the little victims.

> With full knowledge and understanding they themselves offered up their own children, and those who had no children would buy little ones from poor people and cut their throats as if they were so many lambs or young birds; meanwhile the mother stood by without a tear or moan; but should she utter a single moan or let fall a single tear, she had to forfeit the money, and her child was sacrificed nevertheless; and the whole area before the statue was filled with a loud noise of flutes and drums that the cries of wailing should not reach the ears of the people.[14]

How could they perpetrate such horrors? They could harden themselves to do it only because they thought the consequences of failing to do it were worse. They believed that the fortunes of their society depended on it. Their relationship to the gods was purely transactional, a deal exchanging the death of some for the survival of the rest. How serious a business this was is illustrated in one account of child sacrifices in Carthage.

---

14. Plutarch, De *Superstitione*, in *Moralia* 2:495 (Loeb Classical Library,1911).

They also alleged that Cronus had turned against them inasmuch as in former times they had been accustomed to sacrifice to this god the noblest of their sons, but more recently, secretly buying and nurturing children, they had sent these to the sacrifice. . . . When they had given thought to these things and saw their enemy encamped before their walls, they were filled with superstitious dread, for they believed that they had neglected the honours of the gods that had been established by their fathers. In their zeal to make amends for their omission, they selected two hundred of the noblest children and sacrificed them publicly; and others who were under suspicion sacrificed themselves voluntarily, in number not less than three hundred.[15]

What might give rise to such a horrid practice would be harder for us to grasp if we did not have the fact of the Holocaust in our own history. If we did not know of other genocides even more recent—in the former Yugoslavia in the 1990s, in Rwanda early in the current century, in Syria and Myanmar even as I write. I may not understand the bloody worship of Moloch three thousand years ago, but neither do I understand the atrocities of the Third Reich, not yet a century behind us. Vivid in the living memory of some still with us today are modern people living modern lives, driving modern cars, listening to symphonies on

---

15. Diodorus Siculus, Library of History, Book XX, Chapter 14, 4–6. Loeb Classical Edition 10:179.

modern radios—who also gassed and incinerated other modern people by the millions. The worship of Moloch is far away from us now, but it is not the only barbarity in human history.

Archeological evidence enables us to describe such atrocities in the countries neighboring ancient Israel—among the Ammonites, in Babylon, in Carthage. The second book of Kings reports that the king of the Moabites sacrificed his own son and heir on the city wall when he saw that the battle against Israel had gone against him. Examination of our own Scriptures, however, forces us to confront the fact that it wasn't just the neighbors who committed them. The Israelites did, too, at a certain time in their ancient history. We know this because of the prophetic voices that were raised against the practice, which would not have been needed if it were not taking place.

> When you come into the land that the LORD your God is giving you, you must not learn to imitate the abhorrent practices of those nations. No one shall be found among you who makes a son or daughter pass through fire, or who practices divination, or is a soothsayer, or an augur, or a sorcerer, or one who casts spells, or who consults ghosts or spirits, or who seeks oracles from the dead. For whoever does these things is abhorrent to the Lord; it is because of such abhorrent practices that the Lord your God is driving them out before you. You must remain completely loyal to the LORD your God.[16]

---

16. Deut. 18:9–13 (KJV).

You shall not give any of your offspring to sacrifice them to Molech, and so profane the name of your God: I am the Lord.[17]

Any of the people of Israel, or of the aliens who reside in Israel, who give any of their offspring to Molech shall be put to death; the people of the land shall stone them to death.[18]

I myself will set my face against them, and will cut them off from the people, because they have given of their offspring to Molech, defiling my sanctuary and profaning my holy name.[19]

And if the people of the land should ever close their eyes to them, when they give of their offspring to Molech, and do not put them to death, I myself will set my face against them and against their family, and will cut them off from among their people, them and all who follow them in prostituting themselves to Molech.[20]

Ahaz was twenty years old when he began to reign; he reigned sixteen years in Jerusalem. He did not do what was right in the sight of the Lord his God, as his ancestor David had done, but he

---

17. Lev. 18:21 (KJV).
18. Lev. 20:2 (KJV).
19. Lev. 20:3 (KJV).
20. Lev. 20:4–5 (KJV).

walked in the way of the kings of Israel. He even made his son pass through fire, according to the abominable practices of the nations whom the Lord drove out before the people of Israel. He sacrificed and made offerings on the high places, on the hills, and under every green tree.[21]

He made his son pass through fire; he practiced soothsaying and augury, and dealt with mediums and with wizards. He did much evil in the sight of the LORD, provoking him to anger.[22]

He defiled Topheth, which is in the valley of Ben-hinnom, so that no one would make a son or a daughter pass through fire as an offering to Molech.[23]

They built the high places of Baal in the valley of the son of Hinnom, to offer up their sons and daughters to Molech, though I did not command them, nor did it enter my mind that they should do this abomination, causing Judah to sin.[24]

I defiled them through their very gifts, in their offering up all their firstborn, in order that I

21. 2 Kings 16:2–4 (KJV).
22. 2 Kings 21:6 (KJV).
23. 2 Kings 23:10 (KJV).
24. Jer. 32:35 (KJV).

might horrify them, so that they might know that I am the LORD.[25]

When you offer your gifts and make your children pass through the fire, you defile yourselves with all your idols to this day. And shall I be consulted by you, O house of Israel? As I live, says the LORD GOD, I will not be consulted by you.[26]

For they have committed adultery, and blood is on their hands; with their idols they have committed adultery; and they have even offered up to them for food the children whom they had borne to me.[27]

We also know it, and more directly, in two stories: the aborted sacrifice of Isaac by his father Abraham in the book of Genesis, and the sacrifice of the daughter of Jephthah in the book of Judges.

Abraham's near sacrifice of Isaac is the more well-known of the two. You know it: God commands Abraham to take his son to Mt. Moriah and sacrifice him there. Without questioning, Abraham sets out with Isaac, some servants, and a donkey carrying the wood for the fire. As they near the mountaintop, the two go on ahead, Isaac now carrying the wood for the fire upon his own back. He does not yet know the full nature of their errand.

---

25. Ezek. 20:26 (KJV).
26. Ezek. 20:31 (KJV).
27. Ezek. 23:37 (KJV).

Isaac said to his father Abraham, "Father!" And he said, "Here I am, my son." He said, "The fire and the wood are here, but where is the lamb for a burnt offering?" Abraham said, "God himself will provide the lamb for a burnt offering, my son." So the two of them walked on together.

When they came to the place that God had shown him, Abraham built an altar there and laid the wood in order. He bound his son Isaac, and laid him on the altar, on top of the wood. Then Abraham reached out his hand and took the knife to kill his son. But the angel of the LORD called to him from heaven, and said, "Abraham, Abraham!" And he said, "Here I am." He said, "Do not lay your hand on the boy or do anything to him; for now I know that you fear God, since you have not withheld your son, your only son, from me." And Abraham looked up and saw a ram, caught in a thicket by its horns. Abraham went and took the ram and offered it up as a burnt offering instead of his son.[28]

The story of Jephthah and his daughter may not be as familiar to you. Jephthah was one of the judges, the military leaders who governed the tribes in the days after the Exodus but before there were kings in Israel. Convinced that this was the land God had promised to them, the Israelites waged war

28. Gen. 22:7–13.

against the peoples who were already living there for possession of it. Leading the Israelites in one such battle, Jephthah made a vow: if God gave him the victory, he would sacrifice the first person who came out of his house to greet him upon his return. That person turned out to be his own beloved daughter.

> When he saw her, he tore his clothes, and said, "Alas, my daughter! You have brought me very low; you have become the cause of great trouble to me. For I have opened my mouth to the LORD, and I cannot take back my vow." She said to him, "My father, if you have opened your mouth to the LORD, do to me according to what has gone out of your mouth, now that the LORD has given you vengeance against your enemies, the Ammonites." And she said to her father, "Let this thing be done for me: Grant me two months, so that I may go and wander on the mountains, and bewail my virginity, my companions and I." "Go," he said and sent her away for two months. So she departed, she and her companions, and bewailed her virginity on the mountains. At the end of two months, she returned to her father, who did with her according to the vow he had made. She had never slept with a man.[29]

Although horrified commentators ever since have seen the story as an object lesson about the folly of making foolish vows, the writer himself does not condemn Jephthah

---

29. Judg. 11:35–39.

or his vow. Neither does his daughter, who accepts her fate. As frank as the biblical writers usually are about identifying this or that ruler as virtuous or sinful, nothing in that regard is said about Jephthah. Perhaps the irony of the story speaks for itself. But it may also be that the idea of offering an innocent young person as a sacrifice was not foreign to them. The matter-of-fact reporting of this tale, as well as the outright admiration accorded the terrible story of Abraham and Isaac, tells us that human sacrifice was not unthinkable to our ancient forebears. The nature of propitiatory sacrifice demands that the offering be valuable, something costly to the one offering the sacrifice. An animal must be perfect and without blemish. Valuable in its perfection and valuable, also, in its potential—it is a lamb that is sacrificed, not an elderly sheep: an animal whose wool would have been valuable for years to come, who might be expected to sire or birth many offspring and who, in the end, would also have been valuable for food. A sacrifice to God must be a true sacrifice, something that costs.

Child sacrifice, in view of this progression of value, makes a certain terrible sense: what would cost me more than sacrificing the life of my first-born child? Again and again, in times of true calamity, the people of Israel were tempted to practice it and did so, not only during the period of the judges but also into and through the more sophisticated era of David's successors. Ultimately, it came to an explicit end in the seventh century BCE with the reforms of King Josiah, in which the temple at Jerusalem was cleansed of images relating to the worship of other gods, and the use of hill shrines (a frequent place of such sacrifices) was forbidden.

Thus, the cult of animal sacrifice assumed primary importance, though it had existed concurrently with the rarer practice of human sacrifice in the hill places from the beginning. Animal sacrifice was the liturgical centerpiece of worship in the temple for a thousand years, from the complex's construction in 957 BCE through its destruction by the Babylonians and its rebuilding, until its final destruction by the Romans in 70 CE. It was over this practice that the priests and Levites presided. The equipment for use by the priests was elaborate and various—it included copper pots, shovels for the coals of fire, ceremonial knives, many gold and silver bowls of various sizes for various purposes, all related to the killing of animals. This was the temple worship Jesus knew. Mary and Joseph brought him to the temple when he was a few days old, and they brought with them two doves for the sacrifice, the prescribed offering for a family of modest means.[30]

The sacrificial lamb. The scapegoat. The propitiation for our sins. Is this who Jesus is? Certainly it is a theme in our tradition. The story of Abraham and Isaac is one of those suggested for reading at the Great Vigil of Easter. When we hear it there, it is not the Harrowing of Hell that comes to mind, but what precedes it: the sacrifice of the innocent. In Abraham's case, moreover, it is not even an offering for sin—the sacrifice

---

30. Luke 2:22–23

of Isaac was only to be a test of his father's devotion to God.

Though it is referenced frequently in our worship, the idea of the Atonement has fallen on hard times in recent years. It has seemed to many to enshrine the notion of a bloodthirsty and vengeful God, and some have objected vehemently.

> The Church's fixation on the death of Jesus as the universal saving act must end, and the place of the cross must be reimagined in Christian faith. Why? Because of the cult of suffering and the vindictive God behind it . . . Jesus' sacrifice was to appease an angry God. Penal substitution was the name of this vile doctrine.[31]

> I see God as a presence and a power that leads to expanded life, expanded love and expanded being, and even the experience of an expanded consciousness. Atonement is not the word to characterize this understanding of either God or life. So, rather than worrying about whether God can be understood in terms of atonement, I would prefer to remove atonement from the Christian vocabulary altogether.[32]

If Bishop Spong were to get his wish, and Christians permanently left off considering the crucifixion as atonement,

---

31. Alan Jones, *Reimagining Christianity: Reconnect Your Spirit without Disconnecting Your Mind* (Hoboken, NJ: Wiley, 2004), 168.
32. John Shelby Spong, in the blog *Progressive Christianity*, 2.13.2014.

a punishment Christ received when it was rightfully ours, what would happen to our memory of Jesus as victim? Would we find it empty of meaning? Might we not do what some early Christians did, revise our understanding of his significance to eliminate his death as an unwelcome embarrassment, like the Docetists of the first century? Like mainstream Islamic thought does to this day? Is substitutionary sacrifice the only sense in which we can consider his humiliating death?

Once I was flying from New York to Los Angeles. It was a long flight, and I was looking forward to a chance to read my book in peace. This was not to be—the young man in the seat next to mine had his Bible open on his lap, and we were barely airborne before he began to witness to me about Jesus. The crucifixion, in particular, was his theme that morning. Did I know why Jesus had to be crucified? Why he couldn't have died some other kind of death?

*Why was that,* I asked, with a reluctance I hoped did not show.

*Jesus had to be crucified*, he said, *because crucifixion is the worst kind of death anybody could die. It's worse than any other. Jesus took upon himself the worst of all possible deaths for our sake.*

I thought about what he said. The anniversary of the Jonestown massacre had been in the news that morning, that insane moment in which hundreds of parents poisoned their own children and then themselves, all of them expiring in an agony of vomiting, seizures and then respiratory failure. A neighbor of ours had recently died of an especially ruthless form of cancer at the age of fifty-two. I thought of the millions of people incinerated by the Nazis. I thought of hanging. Was crucifixion really the worst kind of death anyone could endure? It seemed to me that competition for that particular distinction was pretty fierce.

And why was its horror the central fact about Jesus's death? Something about this conversation—well, it wasn't really a conversation, it was more like a soliloquy—seemed distinctly off. I knew the Bible better than the young man thought I did, and I knew he hadn't gotten his idea that we could rank methods of capital punishment there. Still, there he sat, his Bible open on his lap.

Jesus the victim. His death isn't redemptive because it is worse than ours. Or because it is *instead* of ours. Jesus's death is redemptive because it IS ours. It is part of the intimacy of incarnation, in which all of life—including its ending, however it comes—is redeemed in the timeless embrace of heaven and earth. English speakers sometimes conjure with the word "atonement" in just this way, making it "at-ONE-ment": the death of Jesus is part of his *oneness* with us. Though this works only in the English language, it is not without value. It expresses an idea of the atonement that does not depend on our embracing a sadistic God.

But what if we were to return to the favorite resurrection image of the first several Christian centuries? To the Harrowing? What if the powerful hands of Jesus, still bearing the bloody prints of iron nails hammered into them, reach into the yawning gate of hell and haul people out? Haul *everyone* out? What if that action were not just one about the past, about the sacrifice of one perfect man balancing out the countless misdeeds of those long dead? What if Christ harrows hell in—and for the sake of—the whole of time, not just one slice of it? So then, it would be *time itself* that is harrowed, not hell, all of us hauled mightily out of it and into the timelessness of existence as it really is. What if it is *this* restoration he brings about: the unification of past, present and future in one timeless moment of complete existence? What if injury and remedy are both present in the same divine and human instant, not strung out in a sad line of human *befores* and *afters*, the way they seem to us to be? What if it is in this way that Jesus dies for us: not as a scapegoat, but as one in whom we live now, every day of his life and every day of ours—live now, and have always lived?

If we thought in this way, we certainly would not have the luxury of ignoring his death—a death we know well, a variation of which we will one day endure ourselves. Already do, though it always seems shelved in the future to us. We could not deny our own end, as we struggle vainly to do all our lives. The brevity of the life we know would no longer be the tragedy we think it is now; its harshness would no longer be the last word. Neither would its beauty, of course—both ugly and lovely would be one moment. Both loss and gain. Both joy and sorrow.

There would be no *duration*. Not here and not in heaven and not in hell. There would be no forever. There would be only now. Both life and death would live in it. Remember

when Martha greets Jesus after her brother Lazarus has died?
*Lord, if you had been here, my brother would not have died,*
she said. He engages her:

> Jesus said to her, "Your brother will rise again."
> Martha said to him, "I know that he will rise again
> in the resurrection on the last day." Jesus said to
> her, "I am the resurrection and the life. Those who
> believe in me, even though they die, will live, and
> everyone who lives and believes in me will never
> die. Do you believe this?"[33]

But Lazarus is already dead. He's been dead for four days.
Jesus isn't talking about not dying. *Even though they die, they
will live.*

Mary and other friends of the family arrive. They all go to
the tomb of Lazarus, all of them weeping. Jesus also begins to
weep. He is "greatly disturbed" and "deeply moved." Love and
death combine in this raising of his dead friend; Jesus lives
in both of them—and the people looking on comment on
both, some marveling at how Jesus loves his friend and others
demanding that he show his lordship over death.

> So the Jews said, "See how he loved him!" But some
> of them said, "Could not he who opened the eyes
> of the blind man have kept this man from dying?"

---

33. John 11:23–26. The entire story continues to verse 45.

All the sorrow of bereavement is present. So is the anger. But we are about to witness a moment that combines both. *Jesus said to her, "Did I not tell you that if you believed, you would see the glory of God?"*

We won't see Jesus rush to his side to save him from dying—Lazarus has died. What we will see is the glory of God.

> So they took away the stone. And Jesus looked upward and said, "Father, I thank you for having heard me. I knew that you always hear me, but I have said this for the sake of the crowd standing here, so that they may believe that you sent me." When he had said this, he cried with a loud voice, "Lazarus, come out!" The dead man came out, his hands and feet bound with strips of cloth, and his face wrapped in a cloth. Jesus said to them, "Unbind him, and let him go."

What is the glory of God? Perhaps it is the presence of both love and death at the same time, the simultaneous reality of joy and sorrow. We do not hear of Lazarus again in the Gospel of John.[34] He will not, after his resuscitation, go on to live forever—he will be the man who dies twice. His raising undoes no law of mortality. He emerges from his

---

34. Lazarus's life goes on, though, in Christian folklore, as follows: he became a priest, bringing the bread of the Eucharist daily to his sister Mary, his sister Martha, Mary Magdalene, and Mary the mother of Jesus, who lived in a cave in the south of France and ate no other food.

tomb still bound in his winding sheet—you recall that Jesus will leave his behind, risen in the very house of death. It is at his command that a dead man walks back into the sunshine of life, still bound.

Perhaps it is a sign of our unbinding.

# The Only Cross You Choose Is the One Around Your Neck

I would just rest a minute. Just a few minutes. Even ten minutes would help.

Eighteen-wheelers hurtled past my little car in the dark, passing me on both sides: Their bulk and their speed rattled me, physically and psychologically: it felt like they were closer than they were. The roadway was wet from the rain. I drove more and more slowly, with the result that more and more of the monsters had to overtake me.

And, most dangerous of all, I was weary. The highway stretched hypnotically before me. Once in a while, I felt the gravelly pull of its shoulder—I was weaving. A tired driver is as dangerous as a drunken one. Behind the wheel of a car, they're pretty much the same thing.

"I'm going to stop for a while and take a rest," I said into the cell phone to a faraway Q. He was already in bed. "Just wanted you to know that I'll be even later."

"Thanks for calling," he said. "Pull as far over to the side of the road as you can."

But that wasn't very far. I sat in the dark car, hazard lights flashing and the seat reclined so I could lie back and rest. The little car shook when a truck went by; with each one, a slice of fear: what if he, too, is tired, and veers off the roadway and slams into me? But my weariness conquered my fear, and I slept.

Flashing red and blue lights behind me, up close. I fumbled with the window openers—whatever happened to plain old windup windows?—and opened the wrong one. The policeman tapped upon the other window. I opened it and began to apologize.

"Everything all right?"

I explained about being tired and afraid of falling asleep at the wheel and needing to rest. "That's fine, Ma'am," he said kindly. "Be careful."

The sermon had been about readiness for death. About the Cross—today is Holy Cross Day—and what it gives us. About fear of death and trust in God. Not trust in God that we won't die, although that's what we always think trust in God must mean. Why we think that, I don't know. Everyone who has ever believed has died.

It was about trust in God that takes us up to the door of death and helps us walk through it. Maybe you expect your cross, see it coming from far away: a grim prognosis with a time line. Maybe yours comes upon you in an instant: speeding tons of steel knocking you into the next world in an unready instant. The only cross you choose is the one you wear around your neck. We don't choose our real ones.

The policeman drove off. I straightened myself up a bit and set out down the road. I had slept enough: the road didn't waver in front of me anymore. The shoulder didn't drag at me. The sky around me was dark, but the sky ahead was bright with the lights of the city that never sleeps. I was safe, now, as safe as anybody can be, as anybody ever is. Safe enough to keep going until it's time to stop.

CHAPTER 4

# Jesus the Word

I remember my own introduction to the term. I was little, six or seven years old, perhaps, and we were practicing for the Christmas pageant. This was always the same: children wordlessly reenacting the story of Christ's Nativity. Older boys read the Scriptures from the lectern—always boys, though there were many older girls who would also have been good readers. These were the days before women could read anything aloud in church, even in an Episcopal church, even in the Christmas pageant. But I guess those girls were needed in other roles— one of them would be chosen to play Mary, of course, and she would be the envy of all the others. And there was a head angel, whose job was to shepherd a troupe of smaller angels, all of them girls. I was one of the smaller angels.

The younger boys were all shepherds, wearing their own plaid flannel bathrobes. Decades later, when I had left off being an angel and become a priest, I would design the ideal ten-second sheep costume: a man's white tee shirt pulled over the head and down the child's body so that her face showed through the neckline, with the sleeves knotted at the shoulder seam to hang down in perfect sheep's ears. But this was long ago, and I had not yet designed that sheep suit. There were no toddlers pretending to be sheep in our pageant. I don't recall what we did for sheep—I rather think we didn't have any. There was a painted cloth backdrop we hung every year, upon which there were a few sheep. But no living sheep figures. Just shepherds and angels.

Three older boys were the three kings. These boys needed to be able to sing, since each one would have a solo part as he walked down the aisle with his offering to the Christ child. I remember one boy who sang his part especially well: he was bit rough, a boy who hardly ever smiled. Some kids were afraid of him. But he surprised us all with his beautiful voice and kingly demeanor. His mother, I learned when I grew up, had had a terrible drinking problem for years, and in a few more would die in a car crash, leaving behind a husband and four children. No wonder he seldom smiled.

> In the beginning was the Word, and the Word
>     was with God,
> and the Word was God. The same was in the
>     beginning with God.
> All things were made by him; and without him
>     was not anything made that was made.
> In him was life; and the life was the light of men.
> And the light shineth in darkness; and the dark-
>     ness comprehended it not.

There was a man sent from God, whose name
   was John.
The same came for a witness, to bear witness to
   the Light,
that all men through him might believe.
He was not that Light, but was sent to bear witness of that Light.
That was the true Light,
which lighteth every man that cometh into the
   world.
He was in the world,
and the world was made by him, and the world
   knew him not.
He came unto his own, and his own received
   him not.
But as many as received him,
to them gave he power to become the sons of God,
even to them that believe on his name,
Which were born, not of blood,
nor of the will of the flesh, nor of the will of
   man, but of God.

This was how the pageant ended, the same way every
year. After the shepherds and the angels had departed, after
the kings had given their gifts, after Mary had sat very still
for all three verses of "Silent Night" while we all watched her
ponder things in her heart, these Elizabethan words from the
prologue to the Gospel of John. John, in which there were no
shepherds, no angels, no baby Jesus, no Joseph. John, who

draws us away from the manger, away from Bethlehem, away from the Holy Land, away from the earth—out, out into the mysterious universe, out into the mystery of time and the creation of everything that is.

> And the Word was made flesh, and dwelt among us, and we beheld his glory, the glory as of the only begotten of the Father, full of grace and truth.[1]

As young as I was, I thought this verse was as beautiful then as I do now. "Full of grace and truth." I myself longed to be graceful, a ballerina. The Word was like that, full of grace and truth.

I don't think I knew then that the Word and Jesus were the same entity—that's a pretty sophisticated concept. But then again, maybe I *did* know–when I close my eyes now and see all of us again in that little church, see the backdrop and the children and the candles, I hear it: *The Word was made flesh and dwelt among us.* I hear the wonder of it even now as I watch us, and so I must have felt the wonder then. *The Word dwelt among us.* There is incredulity in the phrase. Dwelt among us? Among us, occupied Palestine, a little no-account country under the heel of the Roman despot? Among us there in that little country church in the 1950s, among the ladies in their winter coats with bright prickly Christmas corsages pinned to the shoulders of them, among the men holding their grey felt hats on their laps? Two thousand years collapsed into nothing, and the Word dwelt among us in just the same way as it did

---

1. John 1:14 (KJV).

then, it seemed to me. Even then, I must have known that it was Christ. Don't ever let anybody tell you Christmas pageants aren't worth the trouble. Just have each little one bring in a man's white tee shirt and get to work on your sheep suits.

But what does it mean that Jesus is the "Word" of God? Matthew, Mark and Luke don't call him that. Only John. Paul doesn't, either, in those letters whose writing predates the earliest of the other Scriptures in the Christian canon by a good twenty years. So, while the identification of Jesus with the eternal Word of God is ancient, it was not part of the very *first* Christian thought about him. The anointed one wasn't identified in Israel's messianic hope with one who was present at the beginning of everything, and Jesus wasn't either, not at first. He could be the Christ without having been the one through whom the worlds were made. In the world into which he came, he didn't have to be. That thought would come later.

And what about now? We have already puzzled together about the conundrum of Jesus's divine/mortal nature. Certainly the God part of that must have something to do with the creation of the universe, since creation is the work of God, so it is not hard to see why it would become part of considering Jesus's nature.

I remember a seminary professor telling us that in the resurrection the gulf between us and Christ would be no more. Our resurrection would be just like his. *Wait a minute*, I thought—*just* like his? There would be no more hierarchy? He would not *rule* us? It seemed disrespectful.

But yes, it must be just like that. The distance between

Christ and humankind disappears. The distance between Christ and everything disappears, for that matter—everything, all planets and stars and raindrops, all hamsters and daffodils, all composers and all criminals, every priest and every pimp, every atom of everything. All will be in Christ, and Christ will be all in all.

> When all things are subjected to him, then the Son himself will also be subjected to the one who put all things in subjection under him, so that God may be all in all.[2]

> He is the image of the invisible God, the firstborn of all creation; for in him all things in heaven and on earth were created, things visible and invisible, whether thrones or dominions or rulers or powers—all things have been created through him and for him. He himself is before all things, and in him all things hold together. He is the head of the body, the church; he is the beginning, the firstborn from the dead, so that he might come to have first place in everything. For in him all the fullness of God was pleased to dwell, and through him God was pleased to reconcile to himself all things, whether on earth or in heaven, by making peace through the blood of his cross.[3]

---

2. 1 Cor. 15:28.
3. Col. 1:15–20.

The Word of God—when most Christians hear the phrase, I don't believe they think we're talking about Jesus. They think we're talking about the Bible. We stand at the lectern and read to the people. Perhaps it's one of those lessons from the Hebrew Scriptures with a fistful of biblical names we find difficult to pronounce. *Oh no*, you say to yourself as you run your eyes down the page, and you stumble through them the best you can, knowing you've butchered half of them and vowing that next time you'll do a better job preparing to read. Finally you come to the end. *The Word of the Lord*, you say, glad it's over, and everyone else says *Thanks be to God.*

That's what people think we mean when we talk about the Word of God: they think we mean the Bible. Not Jesus.

It is not news that people have different ideas of what the words in the Bible are. We are unanimous in believing that the Scriptures are inspired by God, but that is the limit of our consensus, because we mean different things by the word inspired.

For some of us, *inspired* means *dictated.* The biblical writers were unwitting conduits of the divine voice. Thus, every word in the Bible should be taken literally.

For some of us, *inspired* means that the whole of the volume as we now have it should be considered as one book, and that any internal contradictions in it are not really contradictions. They are seeming contradictions. They can be explained away.

For some of us, *inspired* means that the instructions we find between its covers are to be followed to the letter. It is a manual for human behavior.

For some of us, *inspired* means that the Bible foretells future events.

For some of us—and I am in this number—inspired means that we find the people who wrote our Scriptures doing in their age what we must also do in ours: discerning the presence of God in their lives and history and participating in a conversation that began millennia ago and continues to this day. They did it differently than we would do it. They were not us and we are not them.

It's a bit odd that we have forgotten what many in the ancient church thought the Word of God was—that we have decided that it means the *words* of God. Compared with Greek, English can be a clumsy language. In the passage I remember from my Sunday School pageant—*In the beginning was the Word*—John uses the word *logos*, which we have translated into English as *word*. He does not use the word *lexios*—which we also translate as word. He would have done so had he meant word in the grammatical sense, as in words on a page.

By the time John writes his gospel, *logos* means the ordering principle of existence. The means through which the universe comes to be, and comes to be the way it is.

*Lexios* means words on a page.

And yet, and yet—both words in Greek have their root in the word *lego*, which does relate to speech. Which means that to an ancient Greek speaker, it would make every bit of sense for the Hebrew God to have spoken the universe into being. *Let there be light*, God says, and there is. *Oh, of course*, the ancient Greek speaker would say to himself, *the <u>words</u> of God*

*are the way in which the creation happens and holds together.* So
the words are the Word, in a way. Of course. Nice! There was
much in the new faith that was foreign to him: its emphasis
on the law, the locating of God's guiding action in concrete
human history, the receptivity to both a political and an ethical understanding of who God is. The covenant relationship
of God to the Jewish people was hard to swallow. On a bad
day, he was tempted to dismiss the whole Christian thing as
primitive. But the *logos*—that made sense to him. *Of course.*

But does it make sense to *us*?

We can spend all our time with Matthew, Mark, and Luke
if we want to. We can watch Jesus do important things, listen
to him teach by telling stories. We can close our eyes and make
pictures of him in our minds doing these things, borrowing
Nordic-looking Jesuses from the great painters of the past. We
can even do that with John's Jesus, if we want to: just skip over
the first few verses of chapter 1 and pick it up with his baptism
in the river Jordan. We can stay with the stories, if we want to.
If we want to, we can do that for the rest of our lives.

But we will not always be here. Always, our leaving of this
world flutters at the edges of our consciousness. God-With-Us
accompanies us here, and orders everything we know. But where
does he go when we leave here for that which we do *not* know?

Nowhere. Emmanuel does not leave us—there is nowhere
to go. He is already there.

> "Do not let your hearts be troubled. Believe in
> God, believe also in me. In my Father's house there
> are many dwelling-places. If it were not so, would

> I have told you that I go to prepare a place for you? And if I go and prepare a place for you, I will come again and will take you to myself, so that where I am, there you may be also. And you know the way to the place where I am going." Thomas said to him, "Lord, we do not know where you are going. How can we know the way?" Jesus said to him, "I am the way, and the truth, and the life. No one comes to the Father except through me. If you know me, you will know my Father also. From now on you do know him and have seen him."[4]

We are already there, too, and always have been, though we have spent a lifetime under the sun unaware of that fact. The place prepared for us is another room in a house in which we already live, like the unexpected rooms we encounter in dreams: you are in your childhood home or your current home or your first apartment, and you come upon a room you've never seen before. New to you—but it's in your house, and somehow you know in the dream that it's always been there. *You know the way to the place where I am going.*

Do you remember Christmas Day of 1968, when the crew of Apollo 8 read to us from the King James version of the creation account in the book of Genesis?

> In the beginning God created the heaven and the earth. And the earth was without form, and void; and darkness was upon the face of the deep.

---

4. John 14:1–7.

And the Spirit of God moved upon the face of the waters. And God said, Let there be light: and there was light. And God saw the light, that it was good: and God divided the light from the darkness. And God called the light Day, and the darkness he called Night. And the evening and the morning were the first day. And God said, Let there be a firmament in the midst of the waters, and let it divide the waters from the waters. And God made the firmament, and divided the waters which were under the firmament from the waters which were above the firmament: and it was so. And God called the firmament Heaven. And the evening and the morning were the second day. And God said, Let the waters under the heaven be gathered together unto one place, and let the dry land appear: and it was so. And God called the dry land Earth; and the gathering together of the waters called he Seas: and God saw that it was good.[5]

As they read the ancient words, they beheld the earth in a way no human being had ever seen it: hanging in the blackness of space like a bright jewel, its waters a rich blue, its continents snowy white. We all heard it from here on that feast of the Nativity. My first child was tiny, not yet three months old—I was holding her as she slept, rocking back and forth slightly and listening to the thin voices crackle on the radio,

---

5. Gen. 1:1–10.

across so many thousands of miles. I was so young, so harried, so tired. But even I was thrilled to hear the ancient description of how the world came to be, thrilled that these brilliant men found it still to be the best way to express the awe with which they watched us from afar.

They read Genesis from space on that Christmas fifty years ago, not the first chapter of John, choosing our ancient mythology over our ancient mystery. But both of them tell the same tale, each in its own way: this was our beginning, this Word. Everything emerged from it and continues to emerge, traveling through space, traveling swiftly along with all the other bodies in motion: all the stars, every planet, asteroid, all the space dust, the molecules and atoms, the subatomic particles—all of us. With their telescopic camera they shot the famous photo of our beautiful blue home, arresting it in one brief moment of its long life.

Few of our Christmas cards show this. Most of them focus on the baby in the stable. Some Christmas cards are old masters, Rembrandts and Caravaggios and Giottos, so exquisitely reproduced that you decide to buy a little frame for one of them you find especially lovely, so you can see it all year. Of course you do: we feel ourselves bound to the Earth and her stories. We love it here.

But at times we take a step back from it. In prayer. In dreams. In the intricacies of physics, even, insofar as we can understand them. We have traveled outside its bounds. Much as we love it here, this is not all there is. Mystery awaits us. It stands all around us even now, as it has always stood all around us.

# After the Easter Feast

*I'll have some of the rhubarb pie for breakfast,* Q says.

*That's a good idea*, I tell him. A full refrigerator troubles Q; he likes meals in which everything is consumed and there are no leftovers because the quantities have been carefully planned, which means that the aftermath of a holiday feast is always a little painful.

This year, I bought twice as many green beans as we needed. I intervened just as he was preparing to freeze a portion of the lamb, insisting that he roast the entire leg. We had so many people! *That's murder, you know*, Rosie said as she walked by and saw the lamb. So I guess Rosie didn't have any lamb. I should have left Q alone in his freezer project; now we have enough leftover lamb for three or four meals.

*Why don't you take some of the lemon cake home with you, Gordon? I made it especially for you.* I was trying not to beg. He liked the cake, and so he took some home. Anna liked it, too, and took some home. But we still have a fair amount of lemon cake left, plus half a Russian Rum Cake and three individual Molten Chocolate Cakes. Leftover molten chocolate isn't molten anymore; it's just not the same.

I also got twice as many potatoes as I needed, but I didn't cook all of them. And I think the tomatoes stuffed with pesto will be good in salads, Or, perhaps, chopped and warmed, on pasta.

But Easter was wonderful here. Comfortable and plenteous. Scented with the intoxicating smell of lilies and hyacinths. Peopled with beloved souls of all ages, from sullen teens to Q himself, paterfamilias.

I am still in bed the next morning. I have a cold. The fourteen-year-old granddaughter and niece of friends has lost her battle with cancer. I want to tell the sullen teen about her, about how sweet a gift life is, about how that young girl will not be attending any more family dinners ever again, about how her grandmother longs for her, how her aunt's heart is breaking. I don't, though. She doesn't know her. Not knowing what death really is, she might roll her eyes heavenward and sigh impatiently, and I couldn't bear that this morning.

Several times, Jesus demonstrated the reality of his risen life by eating in people's presence. He broke bread and ate it, and he cooked and ate some fish. He was real.

But the risen life isn't life just like our life. It's not just a reprieve, a chance to continue our dinner parties and wars, our head colds and heartaches. It is a different way of being, life underneath our life, life that goes on around this life, life that has always gone on around it. As sweet as home is here, the risen life is even more our home. We *alight* in it. I think we recognize it immediately.

# CHAPTER 5

# *Jesus the Savior*

His very name means that. *God saves* is what *Jesus*, our anglicized rendering of it, means in Aramaic, the language he spoke. Saved. Saved from what?

From hell, of course, many people would answer. Jesus came to save us from the punishment we merited and would certainly suffer at the hands of a God who, we fear, is more just than we might wish.

Our Jesus was not the first person in the Bible with that name. Joshua, successor to Moses centuries before, bore a Hebrew version of it. Jehovah saves from what? Not from hell: Israel in the time of Joshua didn't trouble itself with the reward and punishment of the afterlife—there was more than enough reward and punishment in the here and now to occupy their minds.

You may recall that Joshua was not always his name. It had been Hosea. Moses renamed him when he designated him as his second in command.[1] People in the Bible are sometimes

---

1. Num. 13:16.

renamed upon being commissioned for some new role—Jesus does it himself, in the exchange now commonly called "The Confession of Peter":

> And Jesus answered him, "Blessed are you, Simon son of Jonah! For flesh and blood has not revealed this to you, but my Father in heaven. And I tell you, you are Peter,[2] and on this rock I will build my church, and the gates of Hades will not prevail against it. I will give you the keys of the kingdom of heaven, and whatever you bind on earth will be bound in heaven, and whatever you loose on earth will be loosed in heaven."[3]

A new name. A new start, with a new authority. A name with meaning for a future different from what went before. A new role in that future.

Our Jesus, though, didn't get a new name. He didn't need one—the one he was given at birth was eloquent enough.

> But after he had considered this, an angel of the Lord appeared to him in a dream and said, "Joseph son of David, do not be afraid to take Mary home as your wife, because what is conceived in her is from the Holy Spirit. She will give birth to a son, and you are to give him the name Jesus because he will save his people from their sins."[4]

---

2. Gr. *Petros*, Lat. *Petrus*, meaning "rock."

3. Matt. 16:13–20; Mark 8:27–30; Luke 9:18–20.

4. Matt. 1:20–21.

Not from hell, we notice—what Jesus will save the people from are their sins.

The phone rang in my office late on a Friday afternoon. Challenging phone calls in the churches I have served seem often to come late on Friday afternoon, near the time when everyone is hoping to get home and begin the weekend. Near the time when offices are about to close for two days, during which it's going to be hard to reach anybody you might need to reach in order *to* help the *person*, and it will probably stay that way until Monday morning.

On the phone was an unfamiliar voice, that of a young woman.

*I'd like to speak to the pastor.*

Two things: I've been at this so long that it no longer annoys me when callers assume that I am not the pastor because I'm a woman. This is just the way it is. And the young woman is probably not an Episcopalian, who would have asked for *the rector.* And one more thing: nine out of ten people who want to speak to the pastor are calling to ask for money. Especially if it's late on a Friday afternoon.

*This is she. How can I help you?*

A short pause and she began. And this call was not about money at all.

*I'm calling to ask if your church allows gay people to join?* That was easy. Many of our members were GLBTQ—maybe half, and it could have been more. I'd never counted. I told the young woman that, and she went on to tell me her story.

She had grown up in a Baptist church in the Bronx. Her

grandmother raised her, and was active in the church—she was a Mother of the Church, in fact, one of the highly respected older women who could restore order among the flock with one look. The church was an intimate community, and my caller and her grandmother were there most nights for one thing or another—choir practice, prayer meeting on Wednesdays, youth group, and all day on Sunday. It was a secure and nurturing place in which to be raised, and my caller had happy memories of life in the embrace of that little church.

Her partner didn't have such memories. For her, church meant one thing, and that was a thorough condemnation of her sexuality. For years, she had stayed as far from church as she could get. But now the two had moved upstate from the city for a job transfer, and both were having to adjust to life in the country. Many things were a shock: the quiet, the open space, having to drive a car everywhere they wanted to go. But they loved their new home, their yard, their garden. They liked their new little town. The new job was a good one. This would be a place in which they could build a happy new life together. They even thought about the possibility of raising children of their own there.

*So I decided it was time for us to find a church. My partner wasn't interested in church, but she said she would go, and that was really something for her—she wasn't raised in the church like I was. If we should ever be blessed enough to have children, I wanted them to know the love that I had known when I was a child.*

There was a little Baptist church just on the edge of town. It was the first church they visited. They walked in one Sunday morning, and never got as far as a second one. The people were friendly, the pastor was a fine preacher, the songs were familiar. It wasn't long before both young women were in the thick of it, getting to know other members, bringing dishes to parish suppers. My caller joined the choir.

And her partner loved it! This was all new to her, and so different from the way she had always pictured church: that church people would be kind and fun, that she would find a sermon interesting and challenging, that she would even read the Bible, let alone find it interesting—all of this was the last thing she would ever have expected of herself. She was handy around the house, and soon she was showing up for the Saturday morning maintenance projects, joking with the men about her prowess with power tools. My caller would send tins of homemade cookies along with her, for all of them to enjoy on the work days.

After some months, the two decided they wanted to join the church formally. They made an appointment with the pastor, who invited them to visit him in his home on a Friday evening. He welcomed them cordially into the living room. He began by telling them what a joy it was to have them, how quickly they had become important parts of the church family, how grateful he himself was for their presence. But something puzzled him, he said. He noticed they had different last names. Were they sisters?

*And we don't look anything alike. I mean, nothing alike. I'm dark and she's really light. She's nearly six feet tall and I'm really short.*

They were taken aback at the question.

*No*, her partner finally said. *We're life partners.*

This was years before gay marriage was legal in New York. They would have been married if it had been possible, but they were as married as they knew how to be.

Now the pastor was taken aback. He was silent for a moment. Then he told them that they couldn't join the church. Their lifestyle was against the clear teaching of the Bible. He was sorry. It wasn't personal, he said.

And the visit was over. The two stumbled out into the night and got into the car. The young woman on the phone with me was in tears, and her partner sat silent at the steering wheel, trembling with rage. *I was right the first time*, she said at last. *Hypocrites. Fucking judgmental hypocrites. They were glad to let me work for nothing every Saturday morning. They were glad to eat the food you made. They were glad enough to take our money in the collection plate. They'd be glad to do it again, if we'd just lie about who we are.* She would never enter a church again. Not as long as she lived. Not if she lived to be a hundred years old.

*Everything was ruined.*

Somebody had told her about our church back down here in the city. I was in awe of her courage in calling me after being treated that way by a church, and I told her so. I blessed her grandmother—I could see that the childhood experience of love in a church community had served her well. It gave her courage to try again after being slapped so hard. I was in awe of that, too. I mentioned a few Episcopal churches up closer to where they lived, parishes I knew would welcome them, including a couple whose rectors were gay or lesbian themselves. *And of course you're always welcome here*, I said.

She asked what our worship was like. Episcopal churches are different from Baptist churches in many ways, but God is God wherever you go. I told her about morning and evening prayer, about the Eucharist every Sunday, about the after-school program and the thrift shop, about the theater. She asked whether we read the Bible and I told her we did. I told her about taking it seriously but not always literally, that we engage it as a partner in a dialogue aimed at discerning God's action in our lives and doing in our century what its writers had also to do in theirs.

This was a long conversation for late on the Friday after-noon of a long and tiring week. But I felt energized as we spoke. Here was a young Christian determined to find a com-munity of faith. It shouldn't have been that hard. But at least I knew I had something I could give her. The church had hurt her, but the church could also be part of healing that hurt. How often do we actually have a chance to do that? How often do we get to mend the things we break?

*Well, I hope we see you sometime, I told her.*

*Yes,* she said, *thanks.* She paused. *Um, I just wanted to ask . . . that is, about your church . . . . Are you saved?*

Ah. Were we saved?

I knew what she wanted to know. Was it our expectation that our people would be able to point to a specific experi-ence of salvation, a moment in which they accepted Jesus as their personal savior? *Personal savior* is a phrase that has always troubled me; it sounds so much like *personal shopper* or *personal assistant*. In the moment they acquired a personal savior, they would know that their future life in heaven was secure. People who had not experienced this could look forward to eternity at a very different address.

This is very real, for those who understand salvation in this way: people who do not verbally and with utter sincerity affirm Jesus as their savior will be tortured forever as punishment for not having done so. No matter what—there are no extenuating circumstances. That we all richly deserve this is assumed, and only Jesus can save us from the punishment we merit.

You must already have guessed that this is not my belief. As hard as life can be, the very miracle of the world's existence and the whole of life in it is too great a gift for me to believe that its author must be talked out of dooming us to a fiery hell. The miracles of healing I have seen and experienced, while they may have been more gradual than the dramatic ones in the Bible, are far too gracious to be the work of so vengeful a savior.

All of this went through my mind in only a second or two, as my young caller waited for my answer on the Friday afternoon. *Are you saved?* I thought of the pastor who could not welcome her into his congregation. I thought of her partner, who intended never to darken the door of a church again. I thought of the members of the little church, who didn't know yet about the visit of the two women to their pastor. I wondered if they would have approved, if they also would have thought it was "not personal"—though there must be few things in life more personal than the choice of one's mate. I wondered if they felt, as he must have felt, that the young women's love for each other was their death sentence. That they needed to be saved from it. That Jesus wanted to save them. Or if some of them may have felt something else, and might have a word or two to say to him when they discovered why the two young women didn't come to church anymore.

I thought of this intrepid young woman's courage and persistence—how, with all that had happened, she nonetheless continued to reach for a rewarding and honest life in a faith community. I thought of her grandmother, of the little church in the Bronx, of the ways in which it was a haven of safety and love in a tough neighborhood. What it taught her. I thought of my church. I thought of myself, of the countless times I have slipped and fallen. Nothing about me is more obvious than my need of a savior.

Maybe we're all living in a tough neighborhood.

*Are you saved?*

Were we saved?

*Yes*, I said. *Yes, we are.*

# CHAPTER 6

# Jesus the Example

We could and should model our behavior on his, we believed. Long before people wore colored plastic WWJD bracelets—WHAT WOULD JESUS DO?—we thought that we ought to be able to apply his teachings to our own life in the world. It is said that Leo Tolstoy did that: gave away everything he had so that he might be faithful to Jesus's counsel to the rich young man:

> And as he was setting out on his journey, a man ran up and knelt before him and asked him, "Good Teacher, what must I do to inherit eternal life?" And Jesus said to him, "Why do you call me good? No one is good except God alone. You know the commandments: 'Do not murder, Do not commit adultery, Do not steal, Do not bear false witness, Do not defraud, Honor your father and mother.'" And he said to him, "Teacher, all these I have kept from my youth." And Jesus, looking at him,

> loved him, and said to him, "You lack one thing: go, sell all that you have and give to the poor, and you will have treasure in heaven; and come, follow me." Disheartened by the saying, he went away sorrowful, for he had great possessions.[1]

I don't know if Tolstoy really did this or not. He has many descendants, and they seem prosperous enough today. I understand that his wife, from whom he ran off at the age of eighty, did not approve of his anarchic generosity—after all, they had fourteen children. So maybe she kept some of his money.

It's not easy, trying to do what Jesus did. Or what he said. He was human enough to be inconsistent, like the rest of us. He talked about turning the other cheek, but then there was that time when he broke up the moneychangers' furniture in the temple. He talked about honoring the commandments, and following them to the letter—but at times he broke some of them. Sometimes he disregarded strict Sabbath observance:

> At that time Jesus went through the grain fields on the Sabbath; his disciples were hungry, and they began to pluck heads of grain and to eat. When the Pharisees saw it, they said to him, "Look, your disciples are doing what is not lawful to do on the Sabbath."[2]

---

1. Mark 10:17–22.
2. Matt. 12:1–2.

The man went away and told the Jews that it was Jesus who had made him well. Therefore the Jews started persecuting Jesus, because he was doing such things on the Sabbath.[3]

Another time Jesus went into the synagogue, and a man with a shriveled hand was there. Some of them were looking for a reason to accuse Jesus, so they watched him closely to see if he would heal him on the Sabbath. Jesus said to the man with the shriveled hand, "Stand up in front of everyone." Then Jesus asked them, "Which is lawful on the Sabbath: to do good or to do evil, to save life or to kill?" But they remained silent. He looked around at them in anger and, deeply distressed at their stubborn hearts, said to the man, "Stretch out your hand." He stretched it out, and his hand was completely restored. Then the Pharisees went out and began to plot with the Herodians how they might kill Jesus.[4]

He said to them, "Have you not read what David did when he and his companions were hungry? He entered the house of God and ate the bread of the Presence, which it was not lawful for him or his companions to eat, but only for the priests. Or have you not read in the law that on the sabbath

3. John 5:15–16.
4. Mark 3:1–6.

the priests in the temple break the sabbath and yet are guiltless? I tell you, something greater than the temple is here. But if you had known what this means, 'I desire mercy and not sacrifice,' you would not have condemned the guiltless. For the Son of Man is lord of the sabbath." He left that place and entered their synagogue; a man was there with a withered hand, and they asked him, "Is it lawful to cure on the sabbath?" so that they might accuse him. He said to them, "Suppose one of you has only one sheep and it falls into a pit on the sabbath; will you not lay hold of it and lift it out? How much more valuable is a human being than a sheep! So it is lawful to do good on the sabbath." Then he said to the man, "Stretch out your hand." He stretched it out, and it was restored, as sound as the other. But the Pharisees went out and conspired against him, how to destroy him.[5]

The commandment about honoring one's father and mother notwithstanding, Jesus blew hot and cold about his own family of origin, and sometimes about families in general:

To another he said, "Follow me." But he said, "Lord, first let me go and bury my father." But Jesus said to him, "Let the dead bury their own dead; but as for you, go and proclaim the kingdom of God."[6]

---

5. Matt. 12:3–14.
6. Luke 9:59–60.

While he was still speaking to the crowds, his mother and his brothers were standing outside, wanting to speak to him. Someone told him, "Look, your mother and your brothers are standing outside, wanting to speak to you." But to the one who had told him this, Jesus replied, "Who is my mother, and who are my brothers?" And pointing to his disciples, he said, "Here are my mother and my brothers! For whoever does the will of my Father in heaven is my brother and sister and mother."[7]

When the festival was ended and they started to return, the boy Jesus stayed behind in Jerusalem, but his parents did not know it. Assuming that he was in the group of travelers, they went a day's journey. Then they started to look for him among their relatives and friends. When they did not find him, they returned to Jerusalem to search for him. After three days they found him in the temple, sitting among the teachers, listening to them and asking them questions. And all who heard him were amazed at his understanding and his answers. When his parents saw him they were astonished; and his mother said to him, "Child, why have you treated us like this? Look, your father and I have been searching for you in great anxiety." He

---

7. Matt. 12:46–50.

> said to them, "Why were you searching for me? Did you not know that I must be in my Father's house?" But they did not understand what he said to them.[8]

> When the wine gave out, the mother of Jesus said to him, "They have no wine." And Jesus said to her, "Woman, what concern is that to you and to me? My hour has not yet come."[9]

By now, Mary had long known how to handle her son. *Do whatever he tells you*, she told the servants. Theirs could be an adversarial relationship at times. But at the end, he worries about his mother like the rest of us worry about ours, and tenderly consigns her to the care of his friend:

> When Jesus saw his mother and the disciple whom he loved standing beside her, he said to his mother, "Woman, here is your son." Then he said to the disciple, "Here is your mother." And from that hour the disciple took her into his own home.[10]

There are those who can be comfortable with Jesus only in his role as moral exemplar. The miracle stories strain their credulity, and the Atonement offends their sense of justice. The notion of divinity and mortality combining in the person of Jesus is too ludicrous even to be entertained. Only the

---

8. Luke 2:43–50.
9. John 2:3–4.
10. John 19:26–27.

ethical teacher is left standing. The story of Jesus must just be a story about how we are to behave, they conclude, and they plumb the Gospels for clear instructions on what we are to do and what we are not to do.

Thomas Jefferson was such a person. Having been displeased for years with the King James Bible in use at the time, he bought a couple of New Testaments and—literally—took a razor to them in 1804, eliminating those passages he considered nonsensical and gluing the rest back together. He titled the resulting volume *The Philosophy of Jesus of Nazareth*. Jefferson created this first effort for his own use; regrettably, no copies of it survive. But he revised it in 1820 as *The Life and Morals of Jesus of Nazareth*, which was intended for general use, though it was never published while he was alive. You can see his first cut-and-pasted edition of it today in Washington, DC, at the Smithsonian Institution.

In Jefferson's Bible, no angels announce Jesus's birth to any shepherds—there are no shepherds. No dove descends from heaven upon the newly baptized Jesus or upon anyone else, and no heavenly voice is heard by anyone there. No devil tempts Jesus in the wilderness. Jesus does not raise Lazarus from the dead, nor does he raise anybody else. Upon the cross, although he promises the repentant thief forgiveness, he does not promise him paradise later that day. And he does not rise from the dead: we see him entombed, period. With that, the "Jefferson Bible" ends.

From 1904 until 1957, new members of Congress received a copy of the Jefferson Bible, printed by the Government

Printing Office, which produces all federal documents. Forrest Church, a Unitarian minister who was also the son of the late Senator Frank Church of Idaho, remembered being given his father's copy when he was ten years old.

> This led to our first serious discussion of religion; it also marked the first time religion made any sense to me. . . . Though I have developed a deeper appreciation for the Gospels in their received form than Jefferson had, this put a bold new spin on redemption, one that has stayed with me. I define religion as our human response to the dual reality of being alive and having to die. Resurrection or no resurrection, Jesus triumphed over death: he lived in such a way that his life proved worth dying for.[11]

The Government Printing Office neither prints nor sends the Jefferson Bible to members of Congress today. But a private citizen does, at his own expense. He is Judd W. Patton, professor of economics at Bellevue University in Nebraska. How is it received? *Nobody has ever sent it back*, he told an interviewer. But I wonder if any of them ever examine it closely, especially those members of Congress who fulminate about bringing God back into government. If so, I wonder what they think of Jefferson's Bible, a Bible cleansed of all its miracles. It is probably safe to say that it is not the Bible they think of when they think of the Bible.

---

11. Forrest Church, preface, *The Jefferson Bible: The Life and Morals of Jesus of Nazareth* (Boston: Beacon Press, 1989), viii.

Just do what Jesus would do. Some people have thought that meant don't get married, since he did not. Because Jesus equates remarriage after divorce with adultery, centuries of fractured families have lived under a chilly blanket of disapproval within churches whose support they probably could have used, had it been offered. He says nothing at all about LGBTQ folk—he seems not to have been as fascinated by sex as we are. But that hasn't stopped those who disapprove of them from assuming that he agrees. What would Jesus do? Usually, we convince ourselves that he would do exactly what we want to do ourselves. A new bracelet: JWDWID. JESUS WOULD DO WHAT I DO.

> The scribes and the Pharisees brought a woman who had been caught in adultery; and making her stand before all of them, they said to him, "Teacher, this woman was caught in the very act of committing adultery. Now in the law Moses commanded us to stone such women. Now what do you say?" They said this to test him, so that they might have some charge to bring against him. Jesus bent down and wrote with his finger on the ground. When they kept on questioning him, he straightened up and said to them, "Let anyone among you who is without sin be the first to throw a stone at her." And once again he bent down and wrote on the ground. When they heard it, they went away, one by one, beginning with the elders; and Jesus was left alone with the woman standing before him. Jesus straightened up

and said to her, "Woman, where are they? Has no one condemned you?" She said, "No one, sir." And Jesus said, "Neither do I condemn you. Go your way, and from now on do not sin again."[12]

Only the gospel of John preserves this moment for us, and many scholars believe that it didn't originally belong there, that it was a story that circulated on its own for a number of years: it does not appear in the earliest copies we have of John's gospel. It takes place in the temple, "early in the morning," we are told—an interesting time of day for the Pharisees to be out and about in search of sinners. They bring the woman there to be judged, and not the man, though the Mosaic law they invoke provides for the punishment of both.

Jesus's memorable choice of words—*Let the one who is without sin cast the first stone*—is more than an ironic dig at the self-righteous would-be executioners. It is a reminder of the whole of the law concerning this crime. Yes, the punishment for adultery was death, something our culture would view as unreasonably harsh. But the death penalty could not be exacted without two witnesses to the crime.

On the evidence of two or three witnesses the death sentence shall be executed; a person must not be put to death on the evidence of only one witness. The hands of the witnesses shall be the first raised against the person to execute the death

12. John 8:3–11.

penalty, and afterward the hands of all the people.
So you shall purge the evil from your midst.[13]

Notice that the witnesses were to be the first to execute the death sentence. If someone made an accusation falsely, the law called for him to receive the punishment he would have meted out to the accused. No *wonder* they made themselves scarce, and that so quickly! Where were the two witnesses? Where was the male partner? Suddenly they were on thin legal ice, and they knew it. *We'd better go while the going's good.*

*Jesus bent down and wrote with his finger on the ground.* Why did he do that? What did he write? And why tell us he wrote something and then not tell us what it was? He did it twice: once when the woman was first brought to him for his judgment and then again after he had rendered it. He remained in that position, studying the ground, until all her accusers were gone, when he stood up and spoke directly to her.

I have always thought it was out of kindness and courtesy to the woman. We are told she was taken in the act of adultery—in flagrante delicto, apparently. And so what would she be wearing? Nothing at all, would be my guess. I think the woman might have been completely naked, or at least so scantily clothed as to be deeply ashamed to be seen by anyone, and certainly by a man. And so I think Jesus bent down and wrote on the ground so as to avoid looking at her. She had had enough of the male gaze for one day. I think he knew that, and spared her further humiliation.

---

13. Deut. 17:6–7.

Folklore attached itself to the nameless woman caught in adultery, as it always attaches itself to Bible stories, quite independently of any scriptural warrant. Perhaps she became a disciple of Jesus, one of the women who traveled with the disciples and supported them.[14] This is no more fanciful than my interpretation of his writing on the ground. Who is to say?

What we can say is that, again and again, Jesus took the opportunity to live and work within the law and also within the larger law of love that encompassed it. Jesus tempered the harshness of the law with a compassion that could take account of what gave rise to a legal issue. Time and again, he rendered ethical decisions cognizant of law but not based solely on it. He based his judgements not only on what the law allowed or prescribed but on hope for a better future for those who infringe it. The woman caught in adultery can go on to live and sin no more. The tax collector can change jobs.

The law is what we have so that we don't tear each other apart. It sets limits: *I won't hurt you any more than you hurt me. If I do, you can take me to court and you will win.* But the spirit of Christ goes far beyond those limits. It offers us a law that stretches our careful boundaries in the name of love.

This orientation toward future blessedness is the spirit of the Sermon on the Mount in the fifth chapter of Matthew. It begins with the "beatitudes," the hymnic pairs which famously contrast the current unhappiness of the righteous with their future joy:

---

14. Luke 8:2–3; 23:49.

Blessed are the poor in spirit, for theirs is the kingdom of heaven. Blessed are those who mourn, for they will be comforted. Blessed are the meek, for they will inherit the earth. Blessed are those who hunger and thirst for righteousness, for they will be filled. Blessed are the merciful, for they will receive mercy. Blessed are the pure in heart, for they will see God. Blessed are the peacemakers, for they will be called children of God. Blessed are those who are persecuted for righteousness' sake, for theirs is the kingdom of heaven. Blessed are you when people revile you and persecute you and utter all kinds of evil against you falsely on my account. Rejoice and be glad, for your reward is great in heaven, for in the same way they persecuted the prophets who were before you.[15]

The Sermon on the Mount goes on to urge us, in the name of love, to surpass mere adherence to law. Jesus invites us to radicalize every obligation we have, both the performance of our duties and the avoidance of our sins. Secret wrath might as well be murder. Secret lust might as well be adultery. Search your heart and work to make it pure. You will never reach the end, for there is always more love to be shown.

---

15. Matt. 5:3–12.

# CHAPTER 7

# Jesus Our Brother

We would spend Christmas Eve with the Community of the Holy Spirit, at their convent in the city. This was new: it would be the first time in many years that I did not have responsibilities at some church or other on Christmas Eve, and such freedom was unlikely to be repeated anytime soon. I look back now, and try to deduce what year this was. Was it 2002? It must have been—I would have been at St. Clements in the years before then.

But who cares when it was, really? Nobody but us cares about the chronology of our lives, and I usually find the chronology of my own life sufficiently confusing that I leave off calculations before I ever settle on when something happened. Now, Luke was different—he cared mightily about when things were, and wanted to be sure we all were very clear about it:

> In those days a decree went out from Emperor Augustus that all the world should be registered.

This was the first registration and was taken while
Quirinius was governor of Syria.[1]

We arrived at the convent at about ten in the evening,
in time to prepare for the Christmas Eve Mass, of which I
would be the celebrant. This was the old convent then, the
one on 113th Street—the sisters hadn't yet moved to their new
one farther uptown. The chapel was on the third floor, and
the priests' sacristy was right next to it. The altar sacristy was
across the small hallway, a tiny space filled with everything
needed for the sisters' many liturgies—daily Communion,
the four services of the Daily Office, as well as the special
liturgies for feasts like this one, the Feast of the Nativity. As
packed to the gills as it was with equipment, the altar sacristy was somehow not a jumble—it was orderly, containing
what was needed and nothing more. The sisters' lives were
like that, too: they had what they needed, and they needed
nothing more.

The glow of candles. The gleaming silver chalice and
paten. The pristine white altar linens, large and small, the
purificators crisp and pure. The smell of smoldering coals,
ready to receive a crystalline sprinkle of incense that would
in an instant transform the pregnant scent of waiting into
the aroma of the divine. I see it now, though it was years ago.
Four sisters descend from their stalls to stand in the center,
a quartet singing in harmony with the rest of us responding
in unison plainsong. I see faces of sisters who are no longer

---

1. Luke 2:1–2.

there. All I have to do is close my eyes. Christmas Eve is like that. Everyone is here.

By the time we were finished, it was after midnight. Even though it was a feast day, Morning Prayer would come soon enough.

The morning sun didn't hit the chapel windows directly, but the mystery and hush of night was gone. In its place, a pleasant anticipatory energy: this would be a day of relaxation, a day without much in the way of work beyond the necessary, a day when even prayer lightened up a bit. We waited in the chapel for the breakfast bell and sang Christmas carols. The old chestnuts, of course, including the one about Jesus our brother and all the ways in which the animals in the stable assisted in the holy birth.

> Jesus, our brother, strong and good,
> Was humbly born in a stable rude;
> And the friendly beasts around him stood,
> Jesus, our brother, kind and good.

My memory is that we were given hand puppets representing all the different animals, and that we made animal noises as we walked down the stairways to the refectory for breakfast. I decided to confirm this with Sr. Faith Margaret.

*There were no puppets, she said. Sound effects only. They started as organ sound effects, and then as the Sisters got into it they ad-libbed. It was impossible to keep a straight face. Cow, sheep, donkeys, doves, camel.*

"I," said the donkey, shaggy and brown,
"I carried his mother up-hill and down,
I carried her safely to Bethlehem town.
I," said the donkey, shaggy and brown.

*No puppets? I could have sworn we carried puppets.*

"I," said the cow, all white and red,
"I gave him my manger for a bed,
I gave him my hay to pillow his head.
I," said the cow, all white and red.

*I don't think we tried to walk while singing the friendly beasts. It would've been a shame to miss any of that hilarity. We did carol as we walked down the stairs from the Chapel to the refectory, but not the same ones every year. Something like* The Holly and the Ivy *or* Bring a Torch Jeannette, Isabella. *By the time we were strung out across three stories we were not singing together any longer. What a mess! But it was fun. After breakfast we'd sing again and the dishes became our instruments. We'd often do a reprise of the beasts because it was so silly.*

"I," said the sheep with the curly horn,
"I gave him my wool for a blanket warm,
He wore my coat on Christmas morn.
I," said the sheep with the curly horn.

"I," said the dove from the rafters high,
"I cooed him to sleep so he would not cry,
We cooed him to sleep, my mate and I.
I," said the dove from the rafters high.

> Thus every beast, by some good spell. In the
>   stable dark was glad to tell
> Of the gift he gave Emmanuel, The gift he gave
>   Emmanuel.

Jesus our brother. I grew up with brothers, to whom I sometimes referred in just that way, as in *The Brothers won't let me play.*

I remember applying to my grandmother for help one day shortly before the Christmas I was seven: I wanted to give The Brothers a Christmas present and didn't know what I should give them. *Well, what do they like?* she asked helpfully. I thought for a minute.

*They like to eat.*

This was certainly true. They were fourteen and ten years old, and both working on growth spurts that eventually would land one of them at 6'2" and the other at 6'4". The Brothers could polish off a quart of milk at one meal without even breathing hard.

*You could make them eating kits, then.*

Eating kits. It was perfect. I scoured the pantry for things they liked to eat. I found two cans of sardines and some crackers. I found two oranges, which I was too innocent to know were being saved for Santa Claus to put in the toes of our Christmas stockings. I purloined two cans of the salted peanuts the Boy Scouts were selling that year, and made a tissue paper package of the Christmas cookies we had been making for some days. All these were wrapped in a lumpy bundle of colored paper and tied with curly ribbon—I had just learned how to make it curl with the edge of the scissors blade, and was eager to show off my technique. There may have been other items in The Brothers' eating kits, but those are the only ones I remember now. Neither do I remember their reactions to the eating kits they received on Christmas morning, but I am confident that they were positive. The Brothers really did love to eat.

I admired The Brothers. David adored Elvis and loathed Pat Boone, so I followed suit, which turned out to be the right side of history. That brother also loved trains, and so do I—he had a set of HO-scale model trains, and continued to love them all the way through middle age, right up until the day he died, corresponding about them with other grown men who still loved the toys they had treasured as boys. He grew up to be a journalist covering—what else?—rails and trucking.

The Brothers both loved to read. They read history, the history of nations and their wars. John read fantasy novels, mystery novels, historical novels, adventure novels. He read nonfiction. He read three or four books at a time. He could usually be found in a chair, lost in a book—you could have set off a firecracker under his chair when he was reading and he wouldn't even have looked up. David read about politics and American history. He loved baseball; he devoured the sports pages in the evening paper. We played baseball in our front yard with their friends. They were kind enough to let me play—so much younger than they were, and a girl, at that. I can see John even now, pitching the ball to me, coming a little closer to home plate so that I might have a chance of hitting it. I can see him patiently helping me paddle in the shallow waters of Deer Creek. Carrying me to my bedroom after I had fallen asleep watching television in theirs. I can see myself, years later, teaching David to dance with a floor mop as his partner. Laughing, laughing. *Jesus our brother, strong and good.*

I was the youngest child. The Brothers were examples. They were older. The Brothers were stronger. I felt at home with Jesus our brother. He felt like family.

The itinerant band formed of Jesus and his followers was not a company of peers—Jesus was clearly the leader, a teacher with his students. But he frequently referred to them as his brothers, memorably contrasting his relationship with them with the one he had with his family of origin, to its distinct detriment:

> While he was still speaking to the crowds, his mother and his brothers were standing outside, wanting to speak to him. Someone told him, "Look, your mother and your brothers are standing outside, wanting to speak to you." But to the one who had told him this, Jesus replied, "Who is my mother, and who are my brothers?" And pointing to his disciples, he said, "Here are my mother and my brothers! For whoever does the will of my Father in heaven is my brother and sister and mother."[2]

2. Matt. 12:46–50.

Jesus had brothers, but he used the term expansively. Those he called his brothers—and sisters—were not necessarily his blood relatives.

> And the King will reply, "Truly I tell you, whatever you did for one of the least of these brothers of mine, you did for me."[3]

> "Do not be afraid," said Jesus. "Go, tell my brothers to go to Galilee. There they will see me."[4]

> Looking at those seated in a circle around Him, He said, "Here are my mother and my brothers!"[5]

> "Do not cling to me," Jesus said, "for I have not yet ascended to the Father. But go and tell my brothers, 'I am ascending to my Father and your Father, to my God and your God.'"[6]

A young man comes to see me. I've spoken with him many times—he is dressed entirely in rags, his belongings in several canvas bags he carries with him everywhere. But he is clean-shaven, his long hair freshly washed every time I see him. He has bipolar illness, and is completely unmedicated, so the long soliloquies to which he treats me make very little sense. Like many homeless people in the manic phase

---

3. Matt. 25:40.
4. Matt. 28:10.
5. Mark 3:34.
6. John 20:17.

of bipolar disorder, his delusions are all about power: he owns many buildings in Manhattan, each valued at millions of dollars. He controls the actions of the stock market. He is the envy of many people, all of whom wish they knew what he knows. I am often struck by the ways in which the frank powerlessness of people in his situation finds illusory remedy in the confused narratives their illness constructs. They become powerful people.

This man always makes me sad. Clearly he is well educated—you can tell by the way he speaks. He had a wife once, and they owned a house together. People at the church remember him in better days: *He was always a little eccentric,* maybe, someone told me the other day, *but he wasn't anything like the way he is now. He's really deteriorated. It's a shame.*

It is. I sit with him in the prayer room. Mostly I just listen to him spin fantastic tales. We pray together. I change nothing in him—God will have to do that part. Once in a while he lands in the hospital, but he knows his rights and asserts them; soon he is on the street again. He is judged not to be a danger to himself or to others, which is what one must be to be committed involuntarily—me, I think having a headful of mad fantasies and no home *is* dangerous to oneself. But the law does not agree with me. I always wish there were a way in which we could force people like him to accept the treatment I know would help him. A constant war between the pastor and the civil libertarian rages within me.

He has a brother who depended on him when they were

little, he says. His brother does not have his illness. He has a wife and a house. He still lives in their home town. The brothers do not have much contact with each other—as a matter of fact, they have no contact. *I was the caretaker of the family*, he says.

I don't know if this memory of the family architecture is factual. It may be. Or it may be just another of his grandiose imaginings, another revision of the sad fact that he has really always been the odd man out. I don't know. Probably I will never know. A colleague here speaks with his mother on the phone sometimes. She still lives in the Midwestern town in which the two brothers grew up. He's been gone from there for years, of course. She must have taught herself long ago not to be frantic about her lost boy—I hope so, though I'm not sure how a person would go about doing that. Sometimes he even talks to her himself. When she asks if she can come to New York to see him, though, he hangs up.

*Come here, Jesus.*

He and his brother are twins. Twins! In the dark, still too tiny to be seen by the naked eye, they swam mysteriously together. They grew together there, occasionally bumping into each other, aware of each other before either was aware of anything else beyond himself. They had never known a time without each other. Perhaps they had a language all their own, spoken only by the two of them, and only to each other. I have heard that some pairs of twins create such a language.

The intimacy of brothers doesn't always last. Jacob fled for his life from the enraged Esau, whom he had swindled out of his birthright. Years later, they had something of a rapprochement, but it was nowhere near a total trust. Mutual trust had never existed between them. They had been rivals from the beginning.

> The children struggled together within her; and she said, "If it is to be this way, why do I live?" So she went to inquire of the Lord. And the Lord said to her, "Two nations are in your womb, and two peoples born of you shall be divided; the one shall be stronger than the other, the elder shall serve the younger."[7]

Jesus our brother. Perhaps we all need him, a brother who did not costar with us in the family drama. Here in New York, people often speak of their "families of origin" and their "families of choice." They were born into the first, in some other town in some other state. Years ago they fled, like Jacob. From what? From guilt? Fear? Or just the knowledge that they needed to be somewhere else if they were to thrive? And they created the second family when they got here: a community of people with whom they could coexist without suffocating.

It seems that this is what Jesus did. His family didn't understand him; they begged him to stop what he was doing and come home. They thought he must be crazy.[8] Couldn't he

---

7. Gen. 25:22–23.

8. "When his family heard it, they went out to restrain him, for people were saying, 'He has gone out of his mind'" (Mark 3:21).

see that he was on a dangerous path? Their love filled them with fear for him.

We know about that love. Our people don't want to see us hurt, so they seek to prevent us from trying things. We spread our wings and they clutch at us, determined to keep us from gaining the air. *Don't go out there. Stay home with us, where it's safe.*

No. We can't. As time passes, you are shocked to find that it's even hard to go back for obligatory visits, for funerals—you dread it in a way that you know makes no real sense. Why the reluctance? Why don't you want to go? What on earth do you think is going to happen to you if you go home? Nothing's going to happen to you—go. People will be so glad to see you.

And you book a plane ticket. But you only stay for a couple of days. You let them think you have something pressing back here. You have nothing pressing here. You could have stayed longer. You're just scared of your old life. You don't really know why.

CHAPTER 8

# Jesus the Revolutionary

I began seeing it in about 1968, I think, or maybe a little before. You may remember it: a crude and slightly smudgy drawing of Jesus's face. He was smoking a cigarette, and he looked a lot like Che Guevara. Like a hippie. He looked like Abbie Hoffman, if Abbie Hoffman had had a beard. But then, lots of guys looked like that back then. Lots of guys in the 1960s looked like Jesus.

I can find it online, I thought, and began to look. I did an image search on "Jesus cigarette revolutionary." I did get a few pictures of Che, and a plethora of other images, but none of them were the one I remembered. I searched on "hippie Jesus cigarette" and got pretty much the same stuff, with the addition of some *Godspell* posters. I tried leaving out "cigarette" and just searched on "hippie Jesus," which netted me the usual suspects plus a few more *Godspell* posters. I thought of "beatnik Jesus," but that was a total blind alley—just bearded guys in turtlenecks and black berets. Nope.

Now I was thinking I might have imagined the whole thing. If you were around then, you probably know what I mean.

I went on Facebook. It was a public post. Surely somebody would remember.

Me: *Hey, does anyone remember an image of Jesus that was very common in the 1960s—it was a very crude line drawing of his face—maybe it was a stencil. A bit smudgy, and he was smoking a cigarette. You saw it on tee shirts, in underground newspapers, etc. Anybody remember it? I'm trying to find it and having no luck. It's for my next book, by the way, which is entitled COME HERE, JESUS.*

I got lots of responses. Some people sent me images, but none of them were the one I remembered. But then my friend Michael posted, sending me the image I was looking for. At last!

Michael: *Here's the problem; he was the Zig-Zag Man.*
Me: *That's HIM! Wait, that's not Jesus?*
My granddaughter: *I'm in tears Mamo?!?!* Ellen,
    Madeline: *Mamo thought the rolling papers guy
    was Jesus!*
Me: *You don't think he looks like Jesus?*
Madeline, her sister: *Oh, Mamo.*
Ellen, my granddaughter's friend: *Omg I'm dying.*

For all these years, I've been sure that the man was Jesus, and he turns out to have been an advertisement for drug paraphernalia.

I was young enough and religious enough and wanted to be countercultural enough to pause before this image. My lingering reverence for Jesus made me feel guilty for being attracted to it, but I was also curious about everything that was opening up in those days. The image suggested to me that Jesus was open to the same things: opposition to the Vietnam War and to militarism in general, the strenuous indictment of American racism and materialism—indeed, to the whole American economic order.

And the cigarette? I think it wasn't a Marlboro. From this distance, with all the water under the bridge since then, all the rock singers and movie stars who overdosed and died, it can be hard to grasp how innocent the psychedelic movement seemed to us in those days. You could enter a new consciousness, in which the categories of ordinary life and work would not apply. A whole other room, one into which no one had ventured before, like one of those dreams in which you are in your childhood home and come upon a door that opens to a room you've never seen, though you've lived in that house for years. A completely new way of seeing the world. Oh yes—the Jesus who turned his back on everything expected of a young man of his time was just the Jesus we wanted. A Jesus who refused to be a stakeholder in normal life. That's what the cigarette meant.

How frightening we must have been to our parents. And I was only on the sidelines. Just thinking of it all now makes me tired.

There were so many things we didn't know. That no

relationship, sexual or otherwise, comes without attachment, whether you know it or not and whether you want it or not. That the absolute freedom you think you want drains everything you do of meaning if you are unfortunate enough to obtain it. That our own desires weren't magical—we couldn't make something happen simply by insisting on it.

And our militancy in the service of the good wasn't magical, either. We looked out over the multitudes of us, the buses and buses in which we came to the demonstrations—we were so many. We could not lose. Did we end the war by demonstrating against it? We helped to end it, I guess. But it would have collapsed under its own wrongheaded weight without our help.

At least some of us were aware of the privilege that had conferred on us an advantage not enjoyed by all Americans our age, aware that many in our age cohort were dying over there and we were not. Some of us were dismissive of them, casual about the enormity of their sacrifice. Most of us were silent about that part, choosing instead the more bracing tonic of anger against those who sent them into battle. It was too soon for us to find our compassion for the young people who fought the war, too soon for us to understand how young they were. How grievous a loss the loss of them was. We didn't even really know how young we were, not really—young people don't know they're young. We don't recognize our inexperience while we are in it. For some of us, it would not be until our own children were the age of the fifty-eight thousand who never returned that we grasped the devastation of losing them. *This was unbearable,* we began to think as we looked at our young adults and thought of those a generation earlier, their short lives receding further and further into the unremembered past.

Sometimes I think that the physical confrontations of the antiwar movement, the tear gas and the pepper gas, the blockading of main thoroughfares, the takeovers of campus administration buildings, the street battles with police officers and National Guardsmen, that all these things were our war games, the mortification of our flesh in paradoxical empathy with the carnage of the real war.

And Jesus? We scorned the meek and mild Jesus of our childhood. I remember people who scorned the patience of Negro spirituals—*Pie in the sky when you die,* a young man in one of my classes snorted, *and in the meantime Whitey gonna roll right over you every day you're here.* Nope. The Jesus who stormed into the temple narthex and overturned the tables of the money changers, that was the Jesus we wanted.

We wanted both of them, actually. We wanted Jesus to smoke a joint and we wanted him to smash up the furniture. We wanted him mellow, but we also wanted him angry, as angry as we were. Like everyone who begins to believe, we expected Jesus to be our water carrier, to be the ideal of which we ourselves might fall short. He would lead us into the promised land of expanded consciousness. He would join us in the street, baptizing our rage with the imprimatur of his presence. He would be and do whatever we wanted him to do and be.

Everyone does this with Jesus. Each era and each person

within an era does it uniquely. Equipped with only our own imaginations and the shared imagination of our religious heritage, we confine ourselves to it at first. We create a God who looks like us, or who looks like the versions of ourselves we want to be. We want a Jesus who is as we wish we were. Faith must start somewhere, and so it starts here, with a God we can imagine. Then we grow, and our imagination grows with us. We wander through Scripture as through a supermarket, pulling what attracts us from the shelves and placing it into our shopping carts. Time passes. We change our minds about some of it, putting something back on the shelf and picking up something else.

Which came first? Was it Jesus the revolutionary? Or was it our own revolutionary selves, searching for him and finding that we could mold him to suit what we were feeling? The idea that religion and politics should not mix has never been universal—their embrace, though awkward at times, has always been with us. It is worth remembering that many of the principal figures in the civil rights movement of the 1950s and 1960s were ordained clergy. Much earlier, both the abolitionist movement and the labor movement of the nineteenth and twentieth centuries spoke the language of evangelical Protestantism. So did the temperance movement, which arose in the middle of the nineteenth and continued into the twentieth century, its influence reaching its peak in the Volstead Act of 1919, which criminalized the sale and consumption of alcoholic beverages—what seems to us now to have been a peculiar intrusion of government into a matter of individual conscience seemed to many at the time to be a needed remedy for a major societal ill, garnering much the same amount of public attention and anxiety as the abortion issue does today.

Today in the adult Bible class our topic was Judas Iscariot. *Hardly anybody in the Bible has a last name,* someone in the class said, *but Judas does.* We talked a bit about his "last name." Simon Iscariot was his father, it says in John 6:71. Some think the family was from the Galilean town of Cheriot. Maybe. Some think that "Iscariot" is a corruption of the name of a first century movement called the *sicarii,* which literally means "assassins." They were militant anti-Roman terrorists. That's tempting: Judas the Assassin. It would fit into the narrative that seeks to understand Judas's betrayal of Jesus as frustration with what looks to us like the teacher's rejection of the possibility of staging a violent revolt. Others object— by the time the *sicarii* existed in Israel, Judas had been dead for twenty years. Yes, but they were around when the Gospels were being written down, comes the reply. Maybe the writers named him that.

Maybe they did.

Some have thought that Jesus and Judas were coconspirators, that Jesus engineered his own martyrdom and enlisted Judas to help by turning him in. So his betrayal wasn't really a betrayal at all. This dramatic idea has gained some traction in literature and film. Nikos Kazantakis's *The Last Temptation of Christ* explores it here:

> "You will, Judas, my brother. God will give you the strength, as much as you lack, because it is

necessary—it is necessary for me to be killed and for you to betray me. We two must save the world. Help me."

Judas bowed his head. After a moment he asked, "If you had to betray your master, would you do it?"

Jesus reflected for a long time. Finally he said, "No, I'm afraid I wouldn't be able to. That is why God pitied me and gave me the easier task: to be crucified."

Which comes first, the revolution or the revolutionary? Is Judas chosen because he already has the sang-froid needed to accomplish this terrible task? Or is he equipped with it as the task unfolds? In class, we struggled to imagine betraying a beloved friend and mentor. Delivering him to a certain death. We talk about the "criterion of embarrassment" in assessing a text: if something is embarrassing to the church but nonetheless appears in the text, there's probably something to it. That Jesus was betrayed by one of his own is certainly an embarrassment. He could have been apprehended by the authorities in some other way. Yet all the writers report his betrayal by Judas. So there it is. However it came about, it is an unavoidable part of the Passion story.

There were revolutionaries in Israel both before and after Jesus. Some of them were hailed as the Messiah, like Menahem ben Judah shortly before the destruction of the temple and Simeon bar Kochba, who led an armed revolt against the Romans some sixty years afterward. His failure triggered the final exile of the Jews into the worldwide diaspora. Pseudo-messiahs continued to emerge from time to time over the next thousand years. They still do.

Jesus was nonviolent. Preached and practiced it. I know, the money changers in the temple. But that was political theater, not violence. Nobody was injured. And there was another bit of political theater in Jerusalem that year: what we often call the Triumphal Entry into Jerusalem.

Actually, the Triumphal Entry into Jerusalem was actually and literally an anti-triumph. You may know that a "triumph" was a victory procession after a successful battle. They are often depicted in friezes on the pediments of ancient imperial buildings: you will see a long line of figures: soldiers, musicians, drummers, dancing people, then the king in a chariot or on horseback. More soldiers. Dancers. Musicians. Finally, and all the way at the end, the miserable captives taken in the battle, chained together, hunched over, herded like animals off to their exile. Such a procession was called a triumph.

Jesus Seminar historians Marcus Borg and John Dominic Crossan describe two such triumphs in Jerusalem the week Jesus was executed. One was the one we remember: Jesus seated upon a donkey, people throwing their garments down in front of his humble mount so that the animal's feet wouldn't touch the ground. The other one was the entry of none other than Pontius Pilate into Jerusalem to ensure an orderly Passover in the rebellious colony of which he was governor. It would have had a large and impressive cast of soldiers, musicians, local dignitaries—just in case anyone might forget who was in charge in Jerusalem.

Maybe the two parades happened at the same time. Certainly, Borg and Crossan think, the parody was deliberate on Jesus's part. It was not a spontaneous joyful outpouring of happiness; it was a signal. *Things are going to change. The Romans may be in charge here now, but God is really in charge.* Like the overturning of the money changers' tables, this was a theatrical act of rebellion. It was guaranteed to get Jesus into trouble. That was what it was for.

So you have to be willing to go to jail. You might have to be willing to die.

> I've looked over, and I've seen the promised land. I may not get there with you, but I want you to know tonight that we as a people will get to the promised land. So I'm happy tonight. I'm not worried about anything. I'm not fearing any man.
>
> Martin Luther King Jr.,
> Memphis, April 3, 1968

Dr. King spoke those words late at night on April 3, 1968. They were among the last words he ever spoke to anybody. If the key word in considering Jesus as a victim is *for*, the key word for considering him as a revolutionary must be *died*. So few modern-day prophets have died in bed; the greatest among them meet violent ends. It is as if their deaths certify the worth of their lives.

Jesus's revolutionary witness might have begun with

overturning the money changers' tables, but it was not complete until he was executed. In this sense, his crucifixion was absolutely necessary. Had he escaped it, he would have remained in our memory as nothing more than a gadfly, if he remained there at all. He would have been one of the many annoyances in the harried life of Pontius Pilate, and nothing more. But the principal engine of nonviolent resistance is civil disobedience: disobeying an unjust law in a very public manner, and then receiving the consequences of that disobedience, in like manner: publicly. Civil disobedience is always public. Not paying the portion of your income tax that corresponds to the percentage of the federal budget which goes for the development of nuclear bombs and getting away with it isn't civil disobedience—that's just tax fraud. Civil disobedience depends for its power on receiving and accepting the unjust penalty that attends it.

And it doesn't expect to get away with anything.

# CHAPTER 9

# Jesus the Wonderworker

So one day Jesus was on his way to heal a little girl who was dying, when he was interrupted by a woman who had been bleeding for some ungodly amount of time—twelve years, I think. Healing the woman took some time, and so the little girl had died by the time he reached her. But he raised her from death anyway, so everyone was happy. Matthew, Mark and Luke all tell this story.[1]

On another day, Jesus was somewhere else and ten lepers approached him and begged him to heal them.[2] He told them to go and show themselves to the priest, which was what you did if you had a communicable skin disease: after an eight-day process involving the washing of one live bird in the blood of

---

1. Matt. 9:20–22; Mark 5:25–34; Luke 8:43–47.
2. Luke 17:11–19.

a dead one, the shaving of every hair from your body while under house arrest, the anointing of your right ear lobe, right thumb and right big toe, first with the blood of a sacrificial lamb and then with holy oil. After all this, the priest would certify your healing, and then you could rejoin the community. This cleansing sequence is prescribed in the fourteenth chapter of the book of Leviticus,[3] right before the part about how to cleanse your house of defiling mold.

On another day, in another town, Jesus was walking with a crowd when he saw a young man's funeral procession, which included the widowed mother of the deceased. Jesus raised the young man from the dead. Once again, everyone was happy.[4]

I could go on. There are eighteen miracles in the Gospel of Mark, seventeen in Luke, nineteen in Matthew, and nine in John, who has his mind on other things. Some of these are a little iffy, like the one in which Jesus curses a fig tree because it wasn't producing figs—when it wasn't even fig season—or the one in which he plucks a coin from the mouth of a big fish in order to pay his temple tax.[5] There are also general reports of his healing everyone who came to him:

> Jesus went throughout Galilee, teaching in their synagogues and proclaiming the good news of the kingdom and curing every disease and every sickness among the people.[6]

---

3. Lev. 14.
4. Luke 7:11–17.
5. Mark 11:12–14; Matt. 17:27.
6. Matt. 4:23.

There are a few nature miracles, like walking on water or stilling a stormy sea. But most of Jesus's miracles are healings of some kind (I include his many exorcisms among the healing miracles, since people of the first century attributed to demonic possession many maladies that today are considered physical or mental illnesses).

Jesus has a curious attitude toward his own miracles: more than once, he orders the people he heals not to tell anyone. Why might this be? It might have been a purely practical matter: several times we are told that the crowds of people who pursued him made it more and more difficult for him to move around the country, and he viewed preaching the imminent coming of the kingdom from town to town as his central duty. But I imagine another reason outweighed that one: the physicality of his miracles arrested people's attention, keeping their focus within the parameters of life as they already knew it. Of course it did—how could it not? *Perhaps*, they thought, *we, too, can find ways to bend this world to our will by appealing to the power of the next.* In the sixth chapter of John's Gospel, Jesus speaks to his disciples after the stunning feeding of five thousand people with a few small loaves of bread.

> "Very truly, I tell you, you are looking for me, not because you saw signs, but because you ate your fill of the loaves. Do not work for the food that perishes, but for the food that endures for eternal life, which the Son of Man will give you. For it is on him that God the Father has set his seal." Then they said to him, "What must we do to perform

the works of God?" Jesus answered them, "This is the work of God, that you believe in him whom he has sent." So they said to him, "What sign are you going to give us then, so that we may see it and believe you? What work are you performing? Our ancestors ate the manna in the wilderness; as it is written, 'He gave them bread from heaven to eat.'" Then Jesus said to them, "Very truly, I tell you, it was not Moses who gave you the bread from heaven, but it is my Father who gives you the true bread from heaven. For the bread of God is that which comes down from heaven and gives life to the world." They said to him, "Sir, give us this bread always." Jesus said to them, "I am the bread of life. Whoever comes to me will never be hungry, and whoever believes in me will never be thirsty. But I said to you that you have seen me and yet do not believe."[7]

The miracles of Jesus do not herald a novel way to beat the system, or an end run around the way the world works. They are signs of transformation, a transformation present now, to everyone and everything—to the entire creation, which comes to be through the very person of Christ. They proclaim that what we see here is not the whole of everything that is, that our own limited world is not the whole world. *Your experience of reality is very limited, his miracles tell us, but it need not be so and it will not always be so.*

---

7. John 6:26–36.

Is this what Jesus thought about his miracles? About himself? Oh, I don't know what Jesus thought. Remember that we don't have a record of his thoughts; we only have the records of what people a few decades after his life said about him. We sift through them from our distant century, but our efforts never rise above the level of an educated guess.

Then again, neither did theirs—we often think that we'd understand him if we had lived when he walked the earth, forgetting that everyone who *did* live then, including those who knew him well, also failed to understand him. Those people were like us—they had to grow into him. And, also like us, they often allowed themselves to see him as they wanted him to be. They created him, in a way. We create him, too. Paul created him. Matthew, Mark, Luke, and John—they all created him, too. None of us can help it. Everything we try to love passes through us. We form it. It is the combined product of its own reality and our need. We can never move permanently beyond this limitation, not in this life.

Does this mean that Jesus's miracles are irrelevant? That the things we read in the Bible don't matter, that tradition doesn't matter, either? Not at all. It just means that all of us participate in the existence of everything. My experience of anything is part of that thing. Read that again: *My experience of anything is part of that thing.* My love for my children is part of them— if I were indifferent to them, I suppose my indifference would be a tragic part of them, too. Most of us have known someone for whom this sadness was true. My reading of Scripture is like everything else—it must pass through me, and I leave my mark upon it.

We can turn again to the healing of the woman with the issue of blood as an example of how we might think about this. Here is how Luke tells us what happened:

> As he went, the crowds pressed in on him. Now there was a woman who had been suffering from hemorrhages for twelve years; and though she had spent all she had on physicians, no one could cure her. She came up behind him and touched the fringe of his clothes, and immediately her hemorrhage stopped. Then Jesus asked, "Who touched me?" When all denied it, Peter said, "Master, the crowds surround you and press in on you." But Jesus said, "Someone touched me; for I noticed that power had gone out from me."[8]

Jesus could feel his connection with the woman in need of healing immediately. Her healing was part of his experience, as his power was certainly a part of hers. Neither was a fact without the other. She would and will forever be the woman who was healed of a terrible condition. He would and will forever be the one who healed her. Neither could be then—nor can they now be—themselves without their participation in this event. It reminds me of the childish paradox you might remember having asked a startled Sunday school teacher or minister or your weary mother when you were little: *If I walked up the stairs,* you asked, *could God make it that I didn't?*

---

8. Luke 8:42–46.

*Oh, for heaven's sake*, your teacher must have thought to herself. But, little as you were, you were onto something. You grasped, if only for a moment, the *relational* nature of everything that is. Nothing can be without everything else. No, God couldn't do that. God is about existence, not the cancellation of existence. God does not subtract—God adds. Every action of ours is now part of the God of whom we are a part: God carries all of us, carries all we are. *He's got the whole world in his hands*, the old spiritual goes. Everything, no matter how small, is necessary to everything.

We might take the African concept of *Ubuntu* as another metaphor as we consider this approach to Jesus and his miracles. *Ubuntu* is the interpersonal and political concept which understands the humanity of a person to be derived from relationship, rather than as the self-contained quality of an individual. *I am I because you are you* is the shorthand way of explaining *Ubuntu*. Neither you nor I can be absent from the equation of us. This is true even if our relationship has been damaged by some violence done to it, even violence one of us might perpetrate upon the other. I cannot injure you without injuring myself.

And the same goes for my loving you. Your well-being is my own well-being.

Seen in this way, the miracles of Jesus are much more than the remarkable parlor tricks of a famous superman. None of them are about Jesus alone: they are also about those he heals. And the two that seem to be an odd fit—his cursing of a fig tree and his pulling of a coin from the mouth of a fish— seem odd precisely because they are not about this reciprocity. You may not even know about them: they are infrequent in Christian teaching. Here they are.

> On the following day, when they came from Bethany, he was hungry. Seeing in the distance a fig tree in leaf, he went to see whether perhaps he would find anything on it. When he came to it, he found nothing but leaves, for it was not the season for figs. He said to it, "May no one ever eat fruit from you again." And his disciples heard it.
>
> Then they came to Jerusalem. And he entered the temple and began to drive out those who were selling and those who were buying in the temple, and he overturned the tables of the money-changers and the seats of those who sold doves; and he would not allow anyone to carry anything through the temple. He was teaching and saying, "Is it not written, 'My house shall be called a house of prayer for all the nations'? But you have made it a den of robbers." And when the chief priests and the scribes heard it, they kept looking for a way to kill him; for they were afraid of him, because the whole crowd was spellbound by his teaching.
>
> And when evening came, Jesus and his disciples went out of the city. In the morning as they passed by, they saw the fig tree withered

away to its roots. Then Peter remembered and said to him, "Rabbi, look! The fig tree that you cursed has withered."[9]

From the context we can see that this curse is a commentary on what Jesus considered the moral bankruptcy of the temple cult—Jesus's overturning of the money changers' tables is sandwiched between his curse and its effect on the poor tree. And here is the story about the coin from the fish's mouth:

> When they reached Capernaum, the collectors of the temple tax came to Peter and said, "Does your teacher not pay the temple tax?" He said, "Yes, he does." And when he came home, Jesus spoke of it first, asking, "What do you think, Simon? From whom do kings of the earth take toll or tribute? From their children or from others?" When Peter said, "From others," Jesus said to him, "Then the children are free. However, so that we do not give offence to them, go to the lake and cast a hook; take the first fish that comes up; and when you open its mouth, you will find a coin; take that and give it to them for you and me."[10]

---

9. Mark 11:12–21.
10. Matt. 17:24–27.

Neither the story of the fig tree nor the fish story are about Jesus's compassion for the people he encounters. That's probably why they are not among everybody's favorite Jesus stories. A fair number of people have never heard of either one of them. They just don't sound like Jesus to us. And yet, there they are. They must have sounded like Jesus to *somebody*.

Even the Gospels, chosen so long ago and handed down to us as Scripture, sometimes *embody* just what Jesus feared would happen: people would be entranced by his works of wonder and forget about who he is and why he was here. His life would be remembered as a magic show.

It must be said that it sounds like a magic show to many people already. Many people pray for a miracle every time they confront something over which they have no control: the diagnosis of a particularly ruthless cancer, an imminent weather disaster, a grievous injury in a car crash. Some people pray for a miracle when they buy a lottery ticket. We pray to be privileged above other people who suffer. We pray that an exception will be made in our case. We pray that the laws of nature will not apply to us, just this once. The "just this once" part is important—our definition of miracle depends on the rarity of an event—for it to count as a miracle, it must be the dramatic exception rather than the rule:

> If Spring came but once in a century, instead
> of once a year, or burst forth with the sound of
> an earthquake, and not in silence, what wonder
> and expectation there would be in all hearts

to behold the miraculous change! But now the
silent succession suggests nothing but necessity.
To most people only the cessation of the miracle
would be miraculous and the perpetual exercise
of God's power seems less wonderful than its
withdrawal would be.[11]

And we hope that if we say "Jesus" a lot we will be able
to order up a miracle when we need one, much as one might
order a pizza. But we don't author the arrival of spring; it comes
on its own. Our prayers don't control the illness of another
person or our own illness—the governing factors are many and
mysterious. It does happen that some people will recover from
a cancer that kills almost everyone who develops it. What is not
true is the idea that we can manage this process. All we can do
is attend to those things we do know, do the things we can do,
and trust in God where the others are concerned.

The wisdom of Alcoholics Anonymous seems to me to be
germane to this discussion of miracles. People in recovery
from the hell of addiction understand their new freedom to
have come to them from a power greater than themselves—
most of them had tried to quit and failed, most of them many
times. It was only when they gave up on their own ability
to control the demon alcohol had become in their lives that
they were delivered of it. The language of miracle comes
easily to many of them who are Christian and to some who

11. Henry Wadsworth Longfellow, *Kavanaugh: A Tale* (Boston: Houghton Mifflin,
1893), 67.

are not, since they know so well how futile their own efforts were in regaining their sanity—in their lives, as in the Bible, the demons are bigger than the people, but Jesus is bigger than the demons. *God grant us the serenity to accept the things we cannot change, goes their favorite prayer, the courage to change the things we can, and the wisdom to know the difference.* Absent that wisdom, there is no health and no peace.

# CHAPTER 10

# Jesus in Islam

*They don't worship our God*, a Facebook friend wrote in a post, in answer to one of mine. *I don't worship Allah! I worship God!*

I wrote back that Allah is just the Arabic name for God. That Arab Christians use the same word. That their God isn't a different God—it's the same one we have. They do believe a number of things about God that we don't believe. But this is also true of her and me: we differ from each other significantly in many of our beliefs about God, yet both of us claim Christianity.

Water off a duck's back. I don't know why I bothered. Well, I do know why: it was because I remembered her from when we both were little girls, and remember how sweet she was, and how pretty. She is still sweet, and still pretty, a truly kind person. I won't turn my back on people because they have grown up to be different from me. But it is not easy, when we have grown in such different directions.

It was a day or two after 9/11. In New York, we were all still pretty jumpy—the backfire of a car engine, the sudden wail of a siren: many of us heard these everyday things now with a new and horrid clutch in the chest that had not been there before, as if our hearts had stopped a bit. On one of those early evenings, I was on the train when two young women got on. Spying a third, they shrieked their hellos, as if they hadn't seen each other in years. Well, it seemed to me that they were shrieking—though now that I think about it, I didn't see anybody else reacting to the volume of their greetings. Before I knew it, I had dissolved into tears of terror. *Please stop screaming! Please, please don't scream!* I begged, weeping, and they looked at me in bewilderment, too surprised to say anything.

Why did I react like that? They were just young people who loved each other and were full of relief at seeing each other in one piece. They were just showing their happiness. I can see now, from a distance of seventeen years, that the young women weren't really screaming at all. It wasn't them; it was me. I know this now. But on that day, at that hour, on that train, I could not know it.[1]

I remember when Timothy McVeigh bombed the Murrah Building in Oklahoma City, killing 168 people. That was in April of 1995. I was a maritime chaplain in New York at the

1. For an account of my own experiences in those days, as well as an examination of the wars in which we became—and remain—embroiled, you might wish to read my *Mass in Time of War* (Cambridge, MA: Cowley, 2003). Depressingly, although the book was written fifteen years ago, most of what brought us into these wrongheaded wars then is just as present among us now as it was then.

time. We had a club, peopled mostly by retired seafarers who could while away their days there.

*Wow, look at that*, I said as I walked through the lunch-room, where everyone was glued to the television set. There on the large screen were the ruins of the building, the front walls sheared away, the ribbons of electrical wires, the twisted steel girders dangling from the exposed floors and ceilings. *Do they have any idea who did it?*

One of the men at the bar snorted. *Who do you think?*

I knew that he meant that it was a Muslim. Some of the guys liked to bait me—they thought I was terribly naïve. But it wasn't a Muslim who bombed the Murrah Building. It was a blond, blue-eyed, American Christian. Tim thought that blowing up a federal building would make us all want to rise up and join him in overthrowing our government. Why he thought that isn't clear, and we can't ask him now—he was executed by lethal injection in 2001.

*Who do you think?*

So it wasn't just 9/11 that gave rise to our national epidemic of islamophobia. It had been brewing for a long time, long enough for my guys to assume that any bombing of a building must involve a Muslim. Muslims were guilty until proven innocent. Even afterward, it seemed.

Jesus is mentioned in the Qu'uran 187 times. The Virgin Birth is included there, and includes grievous labor pains. Of the many ways in which he is mentioned in the Qu'uran, Jesus is most frequently called "the Son of Mary." Over and over, peculiar honor is given to his mother—she is the only woman mentioned in the Qu'uran, and figures much more prominently in it than she does in our New Testament. She is named more often than her son. In the Hadith, the storytelling teaching tradition in Islamic literature that arose after the reception of the Qu'uran, Mary sometimes speaks as a prophet or a scholar might speak. Here, she defends her virginal pregnancy against the doubts of a troubled Joseph:

> So he said to her, "Mary, can there be a plant without a seed?" "Yes, she replied . . . God created the first seed without a plant . . . . Then he said to her, "Can a tree grow without water or rain?" Mary answered, "Do you not know that seeds, plants, water, rain and trees have a sole creator?" Then again he asked her, "Can there be children or pregnancy without a male?" . . . "Yes," she said . . . . "Do you not know that God created Adam and his wife Eve without pregnancy, without a male and without a mother?" . . . "Tell me, then, what has happened to you." Mary said, "God has brought me glad tidings of a word from him, whose name is the Messiah Jesus son of Mary."[2]

In the Qu'uran, Jesus is often addressed, both by God and by other human beings, as "Spirit of God." Like other Muslim prophets, Jesus performs miracles in the Qu'uran. Some of them are the ones we know about already from the Christian

---

2. Aba al-Hajjaj al-Balawi, Kitab Alif Ba', 1:406 (Asin p. 580, no. 187; Mansur. no. 214).

Scriptures, while others were gleaned from Christian writings
that did not make it into the canon of orthodoxy. Still others
appear *only* in Islamic sources, like this one, in which Jesus
converses with his mother before his birth:

> Mary said, "In the days when I was pregnant with
> Jesus, whenever there was someone in my house
> speaking with me, I would hear Jesus praising
> God inside me. Whenever I was alone and there
> was no one with me, I would converse with him
> and he with me, while he was still in my womb."[3]

Or this one, in which the infant Jesus defends his mother's
virginity from his cradle:

> Then she brought him to her own folk, carrying
> him. They said: O Mary! Thou hast come with an
> amazing thing. O sister of Aaron! Thy father was
> not a wicked man nor was thy mother a harlot.
> Then she pointed to him. They said: How can we
> talk to one who is in the cradle, a young boy?
> He spake: Lo! I am the slave of Allah. He hath
> given me the Scripture and hath appointed me a
> Prophet, And hath made me blessed wheresoever
> I may be, and hath enjoined upon me prayer and
> almsgiving so long as I remain alive, And (hath
> made me) dutiful toward her who bore me, and
> hath not made me arrogant, unblest. Peace on me

3. Aba al-Qasim ibn "Asakir, Sirat al-Sayyid al-Masih, p. 30, no. 6.

the day I was born, and the day I die, and the day I shall be raised alive! Such was Jesus, son of Mary: (this is) a statement of the truth concerning which they doubt. It befitteth not (the Majesty of) Allah that He should take unto Himself a son. Glory be to Him! When He decreeth a thing, He saith unto it only: Be! and it is. And lo! Allah is my Lord and your Lord. So serve Him. That is the right path.[4]

There are important differences, some of them mirroring the Christian heresies I mentioned having invented myself when I was young.[5] In Islam, Jesus was not the means by which creation came about, nor was he present at the creation of the world. Jesus's resurrection does not appear, nor does his death. Some Islamic scholars theorized that God took him directly into heaven without subjecting him to the terrors of death, though in his second coming he will die a natural death and be buried. Others had him drawn through the gate of death for a very short time, a death more apparent than real. Some thought another person—Simon of Cyrene, perhaps—was physically transformed to look like Jesus and died in his place. Or maybe, others thought, it was Judas Iscariot who died in his place in that manner, certainly a striking addition to that already complex figure.

The Atonement does not figure in Islamic thought about

---

4. Qu'uran, Sura 19:27–36.

5. See chapter 2 of this book.

Jesus, though he is called the Messiah. Atonement would not be what a Muslim messiah was about, for there is no Muslim doctrine of Original Sin.

The Muslim Jesus is not the Son of God. He is not even the son of Joseph. As far as lineage is concerned, Muhammed knows him only as "Son of Mary." For God to have a Son seems, in Islamic thought, a blasphemous idea. So does the idea of the Trinity—God is one, period. Jesus has been corrupted in the Christian memory, Muslims think, accumulating layers of false tradition that serve to obscure his radical submission to God. They resemble the ancient Israelites in the horror with which they regard polytheism, and sometimes see it in Christian thought where it does not appear.

> And when God said: Jesus, son of Mary, Did you tell mankind: Take me and my mother as two gods beside God? Jesus said: Glory be to You! It cannot be that I would say that which is not mine by right . . . . I said nothing to them but that which you told me to say—"Worship God, my Lord and your Lord," and I was a witness of their actions while I stayed among them; but since you have taken me to yourself, you yourself have watched them, and you are witness of everything.[6]

Jesus is a true Muslim, for a Muslim is one whose relationship with God is in perfect order. It is important for Christians

6. Sura 5:116–17.

to recognize that for a Muslim to say that Jesus is a Muslim does not mean that Jesus is a *member* of anything. Muslims don't think that Jesus left his faith to join theirs instead. They think he understood his relationship to God rightly, and that those who followed him seriously misrepresented him. And so Jesus himself is at pains to correct the many errors which have been heaped upon him—he is *mortified* that anyone would imagine him to be the son of God, devastated to learn that some equate him with God the Father. Not only is Jesus horrified by such a thought, so is the whole creation:

> They say: "The God of Mercy hath gotten offspring." Now have ye done a monstrous thing! Almost might the very Heavens be rent thereat, and the Earth cleave asunder, and the mountains fall down in fragments, that they ascribe a son to the God of Mercy, when it beseemeth not the God of Mercy to beget a son! Verily there is none in the Heavens and in the Earth but shall approach the God of Mercy as a servant.[7]

The Jesus of Islam is a prophet in a long line of honored prophets—Adam, Abraham, Moses, John the Baptist. He is the last in the line before the Prophet Muhammed himself. After Muhammed, there is no further need for prophets: he has revealed God as completely as human beings can bear. The Qu'uran is a sufficient guide thenceforth. As in Judaism

---

7. Sura 19:91–94.

and Christianity, Islamic scholars commented on their sacred texts and the folklore that arose around them. Jesus figures frequently in this literature, as well.

Islam flowered in a world already familiar with Jewish and Christian texts and extra-canonical mythology. It should surprise no one that we encounter many of the same people in the sacred texts of all three. Muhammed did not understand himself to be inaugurating the worship of a new god. He was simply calling us to renewed submission to the one we already had, the one revealed to the biblical patriarchs and to Jesus already. But he viewed the Christian Scriptures as compromised, distorted by human interference. He reckons with and confronts Christian tradition. Muslim historian Tarif Khalidi has described Jesus in the Qu'uran as "embroiled in polemic."

> Jesus is a controversial prophet. He is the only prophet in the Qu'uran who is deliberately made to distance himself from the doctrines that his community is said to hold of him.[8]

In the Muslim Jesus, we see people outside the Christian community doing what people within it also do: molding their idea of Jesus to fit their world. The church the earliest Muslims encountered had grown steadily more hierarchical: Christ was the sole mediator between mortals and God, and the church was the only avenue to him. The Judaism they

---

8. T. Khalidi, *The Muslim Jesus* (Cambridge, MA: Harvard University Press, 2001), 12.

knew remained insular and tribal. Seen against this backdrop, Islam represented a radical "democratization" of the human relationship to God. The relationship is direct: no priest owns the key to it and no sacrament unlocks it. The peasant is as able as the king to enter into it. As exalted a place as Jesus holds in Islam, he is still one among the many human beings called to submit wholeheartedly to God. We can see this in the Qu'uran on occasions such as this one, when he himself is exhorted to a practice of a righteousness he has yet to attain, having invited John the Baptist to instruct him:

> Jesus met John and said to him, "Admonish me." He [John] said, "Avoid feeling anger." He [Jesus] said, "This I cannot do." He [John] said "Do not own any wealth." He[Jesus] said, "As for this—it is possible."[9]

And this, in which his miracles and his teaching are only by God's leave:

> [Jesus said] I will heal the blind, and the leper, and by God's leave I will quicken the dead; and I will tell you what you eat, and what you store up in your houses.[10]

It may be—certainly it seems so to me—that the Eucharist is described here, though shorn of its connection to Jesus's death and to the exclusive ministry of priests:

---

9. Ahmad ibn Hanbal, *al-Zuhd*, No. 322.
10. Sura 3:4.

Jesus, Son of Mary, said: "O God our Lord! Send down a table to us out of heaven, that it may become a recurring festival to us, to the first of us and the last of us, and a sign from thee; and do thou nourish us, for thou art the best of nourishers."[11]

Note the mention here of "the first of us and the last of us," an echo of Jesus's frequent reference to the inversion of the facts of earthly power in the kingdom of heaven (for example, in Matthew 20:16, "and the last shall be first, and the first, last.") A Muslim would have said that the spirit of this authentic saying of Jesus had been grievously corrupted by the church, its egalitarianism replaced by a priest-ridden hierarchy in which rank was more important than it should be in the approach to God. This, of course, was also the premise of the Protestant Reformation.

No, Muslims and Christians are not the same. But God is the same. The new faith thought it important to reckon with Jesus, and its sacred text does so. Muslims honored him in the seventh century and still do today. For a thousand years, they have viewed Jesus with great respect, though in a way very different from that of his own followers.

11. Sura 5:114.

# CHAPTER 11

# *What I Think*

What do I think about Jesus?

I was about ten years old. I was at Brownie camp—my first sleepaway camping experience. I was equipped for the adventure with, among other things, my very own flashlight, which I found irresistible. We each had one, in case we needed to get up at night to answer nature's call—the latrine was a short distance away.

The camp was dark and still when I awoke. It must have been after midnight. Put on my slippers and my jacket, crept to the cabin door, flashlight in hand, and started down the path.

I had not gotten far before I saw him. He stood calmly in the clearing ahead of me, watching me walk toward him. I knew it was Jesus—he looked just as he looked in my children's Bible at home: long brown hair, a beard, blue eyes, a long white robe. Of course it was Jesus.

Jesus looked at me and I looked at him. He said, "Follow me."

"Okay," I said, and went back to my cabin.

This was a real experience. It may also have been a dream—I am no longer sure. But it was real, nonetheless. Real to me. It still is real to me. Whether it was a waking vision or a sleeping one doesn't matter much to me now. It doesn't matter that I was only a child, or that it was so long ago. I have come to think it was my first experience of a call to serve in the way I've now served for more than half my life. Later I would read about the disciples' being called in just this way—*Follow me.* He was The Way. I recognized the voice.

What do I think about Jesus?

I don't worry as much about the nature of Jesus as the polemicists of the first several Christian centuries did. They just about murdered each other over whether or not the Son proceeded from the Father. Even now, sometimes, you'll encounter a person at a church meeting who seems like he still could. Steer clear of him.

Jesus was what he was and is what he is. I don't particularly want to define him. What I want to do is follow him.

It takes a lifetime just to know an ordinary person. Anybody. And even when you've spent a lifetime together, you can still be amazed by a detail of a life that is news to you. You thought you knew everything about him. But no.

*Wait, you danced with Jackie Kennedy?*

Q thought a moment. *Well, she wasn't Jackie Kennedy then. She went to school with June.*

June was Q's late cousin. We were looking at an old photograph of her with Q and his cousin Jack. They were all in evening clothes. It was 1947, maybe or 1948. The three of them were sitting together in a banquette and laughing at something. Jack was a handsome fellow. He would later die of polio, so I never met him. June was a real beauty—she's gone now, too. Q is the only one of those cousins still living.

*Where were you?*

*It was at a hotel in New York. I forget which one. Jack and I took her.*

*You both took her?*

*Yes. Each girl had to be escorted by two guys. Cousins or brothers or something. Somebody she couldn't marry.*

*Good Lord.*

*Well, it was a long time ago. They probably don't do it that way now.*

They probably still do it *exactly* that way.

So, my husband danced with Jackie Kennedy, before she was Jackie Kennedy. We'd been married for about twenty years when this news hit. And there have been other things. I learned sometime in the early '90s that he hid a bicycle under some bushes on the Isle of Skye in 1947 and never went back for it. He walked into the Mediterranean stark naked and went for a swim early one morning when we were in Nice for an academic conference—this I saw with my very own eyes. I also saw him kiss a python on the nose once, at a street fair.

You think you know people. But you don't know everything. People are mysterious. Every last one of them, a mystery. They mystery of them unfolds, bit by bit, over years, but it never completely disappears.

We're going to have to let Jesus be a mystery, too. We'll have to accept the fact that we won't know and can't know every last thing about him. There will always be surprises—that's what it is to be in relationship with someone. With anyone. You have to be willing to be surprised.

But the very fact of his mysteriousness frees us to learn from everyone else's experience of him. What Jesus meant for someone in the past had value for that person and her community, and so it is valuable for me, even if I don't agree with it. The same is true for the different experiences of him we encounter in the present, though this is a *lot* harder to do: it is one thing to appreciate a first-century Docetist, and quite another to interact harmoniously with a twenty-first-century one. But everybody's Jesus has a reason behind him, some human need that is met by thinking in a certain way. Perhaps it is a need I also have. If I can come to understand a point of view about him different from my own and grasp what is it about him that appeals, and why it appeals, I might recognize some common ground.

My modern-day Docetist friend has a very high view of God's power. So does my Muslim friend. So do I.

My lefty Christian friend cares passionately about justice. So do I.

My friend who insists vehemently on the Atonement cares about righteousness. He wants the scale that weighs sin and righteousness to balance at the end. I do, too.

My friend who focuses on Jesus's miracles knows about human weakness in the face of the harsh and heavy burdens of human life. I know a fair amount about that, too.

My friend who sees Jesus primarily as a moral example wants to do what Jesus would do. I would like to do that, if I thought I could know what that might be.

I am profoundly agnostic—less about God than about what I can know. That, after all, is what the word "agnostic" means—"without knowledge." I am without knowledge. I imagine you have suspected already that I am not deeply committed to the Virgin Birth or the miracles of Jesus as historical facts. I don't think they were transmitted to us in the expectation that we would receive them in that way. They are sacred stories, important not because of their facticity but because of their meaning. I *am* committed to the truths they represent. I preach on them all the time. If we were somehow to discover tomorrow that none of them had actually occurred as they are described, I would no more excise them from Scripture than I would the Psalms. If, on the other hand, we were to discover that all of them had, their immense value to me would be about the same as it is now.

I guess I'm with John's prologue: *In the beginning was the Word, and the Word was with God, and the Word was God.*

In the beginning, there is a singularity. One thing. It is energy, but dense beyond all density, saturated with the weight of all existence and all time. This is an eternal singularity, something not boundaried by time or space. This is the energy of being. By its nature, it pushes out against the chaos of nothingness. On and on it goes, bringing being into being against the greedy suck of non-being, pulling existence out of the jaws of non-existence.

The Word is this push. If we use traditional Trinitarian language, the Word is the Son—the church has said for centuries that God the Father created the cosmos by God the Son through the power of God the Holy Spirit. The creation of everything is an explosion of existence into the vacuum of nothingness. On and on it goes, creating and creating as it goes: faster, stronger, hotter, cleaner. The fact of energy becomes also the fact of matter—we have known since Einstein that, in a sense, matter and energy are really the same thing. We ourselves emerge from this identity—we are made of it, as is everything else. You and me and everything. So is Jesus of Nazareth, who both brings about and shares my existence and yours, shares the existence of everything that is. So is what we know as history, and so is the linearity we are naïve enough to think sums up what time is, when it is really only a slice of what time is.

It is impossible to overstate how important time is in coming to terms with the all-encompassing existence of God. Human beings have a difficult time thinking in other than binary terms. We resist moving beyond *this or that, black or white, yes or no, true or false.* But this inability rests on our linear experience of something which is not really linear—time, in God's experience, cannot be the one-thing-after-another line we think it is. If God's experience could be contained on a line, we would certainly not be talking about God. Such a being would be only slightly less limited than we ourselves. God's reality must be different: it must be one of simultaneity, of all ages equally present. God must behold every time and every place, in one moment. Every moment must be contained in the divine present, the steady now of God.

This brings us to the question of evil. Of suffering. Of injustice. If every moment is contained in the divine now, what about the terrible moments? Are they there, too? What about the many evil deeds that go unrepaired and unpunished, about suffering that goes unrelieved? For centuries, our old linear understanding of time has provided us with a place to put these things—evil is destroyed at the end of time, when the line draws to its close and the universe ends. Heaven contains no evil, and Hell contains no good. Lock it all in and bolt the door. But, though this provides us with a balanced scale, it is a balance that leaves us unsatisfied. *Okay*, we say, *it balances in the end.* But sometimes we are not sure it is worth the price. We spin hopeful stories about the final recompense, about just how golden a place heaven will be. But the years of pain drag on and on until then. At times, we feel—with an uneasy sense of our disloyalty to the cause—that a balanced scale at the end of time is not enough. When we add to this our conviction that Jesus demands our compassionate service to others, we are even more uneasy: we know that our efforts will fall short. We know that people will slip through the cracks. We know, even, that our own compassion will fail sometimes. There will be harshness and injustice on the earth. We will even be implicated in some of it.

What I am suggesting—the simultaneity of the reality

of God—is much less clear-cut and feels much less secure than recompense at the end of time. There is no end of time. Recompense is not part of it. What? Wait—pain and loss continue in the domain of God? Why is that a good idea?

Careful. There is a problem with the word "continue." Things can continue along a line, but nothing continues in "now." In the simultaneous reality of God, there can be no continuing. There is no duration. Time in this sense is not *chronos*, the time of clocks or calendars. It is *kairos*. God's time. God's time does not *elapse*. Everything that ever was, *is*. Everything that ever will be, *is*. All at once. No sooner than something *is,* it also *is not*. It is not the case that your mother's suffering, which you watched at the end of her life, must now go on forever in the domain of God. No line stretches out to the crack of doom. There is no *forever* here.

Scripture draws our attention to this in a symbolic way in the post-resurrection appearances of Jesus. By insisting that the prints of the nails in his hands and feet and the wound in his side were visible to others, it reminds us that nothing about the Resurrection cancels out the reality of the Crucifixion. Both are real, one in the ordinary historical sense we know well and one in a more mysterious way. Both have happened. The joy and the sorrow are both present in the resurrected life, visible in the very resurrected body of Jesus, as they were both present in his earthly ministry. When we hear of Christ trampling down death at an Easter liturgy or at a funeral, for instance—*Christ is risen from the dead, trampling down death by death, and giving life to those in the tomb*[1]—we do not mean that thenceforth nobody dies. We mean that death is part of the continuum of existence in which we all participate. Allowing ourselves to consider the simultaneity of *kairos* keeps us firmly in mind that it *is* a continuum.[2]

It would be reasonable for someone to ask what could be comforting about giving up so personal a God as most of us have inherited. Is not this a bloodless way of thinking about God, bloodless and far too abstract for us—a force, like gravity or radiation? Where would we put our emotions in dealing with such a God? Doesn't this way of thinking demand a level of detachment beyond what is human in us? Feelings are important. We are not fully human without them. Am I suggesting that they are irrelevant?

Not at all. But neither are they everything.

I sit with both my feet on the floor. I take off my glasses. I begin to pay attention to my breathing, noticing its in-and-out rhythm. This is the gift of God to me, the gift of life. It breathed over the waters of chaos at the beginning and it breathes in me. I tighten my feet, pointing my toes hard, then flexing both feet. I hold it—hard, hard, hard—and then I let it go. At once it is as if my feet had disappeared. All the while, my breath: in and out, deep, but not hard. The breath of life. I do the same with the calves of my legs, with the great

---

1. "Paschal Troparion," transl. in "The Burial of the Dead," Book of Common Prayer, 500.

2. For a more fulsome discussion of this idea of time and its implications, as well as of the idea of God as energy, see my own book *The Alsolife* (New York: Church Publishing, 2016).

muscles of my thighs, with my abdomen, my hands, my arms, my shoulders, my face. As I tighten and relax each one, it is as if it has disappeared—I need have no concern for it. And all the while, the breath.

I begin to repeat a holy word. Deliberately, I choose one that won't evoke an image in my imagination—I don't choose Jesus, for instance. I use something much less pictorial. Holy, for instance, is the one I use. *Holy, holy, holy, holy, holy,* again and again and again and again. If a thought comes to me, a sensation, a worry, a sound: I repeat the holy word until it passes. There is only the holy word and the breath.

And then I descend, a gentle slide down to the place where I am beneath everything that is, a place that is not a place at all, but a way of being. Everything is there, and nothing is there—it is *all* there. *Holy, holy, holy, holy, holy.* I slide down upon the word, as if it were a road. The word is the way down. It takes me there. *I am the way, and the truth and the life.* I behold it, not with my eyes but with my spirit.

I can stay there as long as I want to. I can return whenever I wish. It is always there. It has never not been. It will never not be.

In contemplative prayer, we learn to tell the difference between our feelings and the reality that transcends them. This reality is beneath all our stories and our histories, beneath our senses and our thoughts. It supports all of them. It beholds all of them. It holds them. We rest in it. We always have and always will. We lose nothing of our beloved tales, our mythologies, all the ways in which we have imagined God. We need not surrender a single story. God contains all of them.

In the energetic stillness in which everything exists, all the walls fall down. The beloved dead live still, not only in our remembered experience of them but in the larger reality of the alsolife—which contains all their yesterdays and is our reality even now, though we sense it only dimly and, usually, not at all. The past remains. It lives here with us, and so does the future. They are absent only from *chronos*.

They are eternally present in the present of God.

No, in my most intimate experience of Jesus I see no sheep and no shepherds. I hear no angels and see no disciples. There are no stories or wise sayings. All those things remain outside these moments, waiting at the door in case I have need of them—they wait there between the covers of my Bible any time I wish to think of them, to talk about them, to preach on them or to allow them to suggest an encouraging, healing thought to someone who comes to me in desperate need of one. I call upon them often. They have never failed me.

But in my heart of hearts, Jesus comes to me most often in deep silence. All I have to do is turn toward him and he is there. I remember more experienced people telling me things like this when I was younger, and I remember that I despaired of ever becoming such a person. *These must be extraordinary souls,* I thought. *Surely these are spiritual adepts. Surely it cannot be so simple.* But I can tell you now that one need not be extraordinary in any way to pray in this way, and that it does become easier to do with years of practice, and that you need not take your own temperature every few minutes to see if you're doing it right. Just doing it *is* right.

*He is the Way.*

My Way, at least. Perhaps he is not yours. But that is just a difference between me and you, between the ways in which we were brought up and the stories we were told and which we still tell, none of which are absolute. It is not a difference between either of us and Jesus. He is all the ways of humanity to God. They are the same Way. This is what Jesus knew.

The silence of his presence leads me to the wall between the worlds and allows me to slip through it. This is what happens in contemplative prayer, so readily available to all of us, so *there*, just for our turning to it. This and all the other practices of a devout life both ground us here and prepare us for a holy death. One day I will slip through the wall, not in prayer, but in death. So will you. So will everybody, the righteous and the unrighteous. The happy and the sad.

On that day, we will look around and see that it is today and it is here.

It has always been here.

And it has always been today.

# Peace I Leave with You

*Peace I leave with you; my peace I give to you. I do not give to you as the world gives. Do not let your hearts be troubled, and do not let them be afraid.*
— *John 14:27*

You open your eyes in the first gray light of morning. For a moment you just feel the goodness of it: the clean sheets, the silence. And then you remember what happened last night. All is not well. You said things you shouldn't have said. Or maybe you should have said them, but you should have put them a different way.

You open your eyes in the first gray light of morning. At first, you forget where you are, and think that you're at home. But the bed is uncomfortable and the guy in the next bunk is snoring. Your wife never snores. You're not at home. You're in a tent outside Tikrit.

You open your eyes in the first gray light of a Syrian morning, and at first you forget where you are. Then you remember that you have left the ruins of your home and are walking, walking, walking. You and your children slept by the side of the road.

You open your eyes in the first gray light of morning, and for a moment you forget about the money. But then you remember everything, that the money is due this week and you don't know where you're going to get it.

You open your eyes in the first gray light of morning, and for a moment you forget about the cancer. Then you remember, and you deflate like a sad little balloon. Peace I give to you, my own peace I leave with you. Life is hard, but peace does not come only from life being easy. Whatever you must face today, I am with you. I will give you peace in your heart and peace in your mind so that their energies can be focused on the tasks at hand. I will give you the consciousness of small joys—the song of birds, the sound of your music, the taste of food, the sight of flowers. I will give you peace, whatever the world dishes out. You will take things one step at a time. One step at a time, you will get through what you must go through.

# Questions for Discussion

CHAPTER 1 • Jesus the Son of God

1. Would it trouble you to think that the Virgin Birth might not be factual? Why or why not?

2. Why do you think Jesus kept his distance from his family of origin?

3. We know that some early Christians did not want the Hebrew Scriptures in the Christian canon. Is there anything in the Bible you would want to leave out if you were compiling it today? Why? Is there anything you wish were in it that isn't?

4. Have you ever had to choose between your obligation to your family and your moral obligation?

### CHAPTER 2 • Jesus Who Knew Everything

1. How do you respond to the idea that Jesus might have been mistaken about things?

2. The chapter suggests that the difference between human linear time and God's experience of simultaneity is important in addressing the questions of what Jesus knew. What is the relation of time to Jesus's "all-knowingness"?

3. Does it trouble you to consider the idea that there may not be a divine plan, in the same sense that human beings make plans—that is, planning ahead in time, before things happen?

### CHAPTER 3 • Jesus the Victim

1. Did Jesus have to be crucified?

2. How do you respond to the verse that begins this chapter? Addressing Jesus, it contains the words "I crucified thee." What do you think of that idea?

3. The church affirms the idea of the Atonement in many places in its liturgy, but we have seen that some theologians today reject the concept. How do you view it?

4. The chapter suggests strongly that a tradition of human sacrifice, especially that of children, was a part of our ancient history. How do you respond to that suggestion?

## CHAPTER 4 • Jesus the Word

1. Do you find the idea of Christ as the Word a useful idea for you personally?

2. Would it matter to you if Christ were a created being? People in the early church were very passionate about this.

3. We often say that the universe was created by God the Father, through God the Son, by the power of the Holy Spirit. John 1:1–11 spells this out, and yet many modern people find it hard to understand or to see it as having anything to do with themselves. Do you?

4. John 1:1–11 is felt by some to open a door to the idea of many possible universes and other ideas arising from recent developments in science. How do you respond to this?

## CHAPTER 5 • Jesus the Savior

1. Are you saved? Have you ever been asked that? How would/did you respond?

2. What would it mean to you if there were no hell?

3. My caller was refused membership in the church because she was in a lesbian relationship. What lifestyle requirements should a church have for its members? Should it have any? How should they be determined?

4. What does it mean to "join the church"?

## CHAPTER 6 • Jesus the Example

1. 1. Do you know someone whom you would describe as "Christlike"? Who is it? Why is s/he like Jesus?

2. The chapter suggests that each age "creates its Jesus" under the rubric "Jesus Would Do What I Do." Do you agree? What Jesus has our age "created"?

3. What do you think of the "Jefferson Bible"?

## CHAPTER 7 • Jesus Our Brother

1. Is Jesus our Brother an image you like or one you dislike? Why?

2. How do you view Jesus's relationship with his family of origin?

3. If Jesus is our brother, can he also be our God?

## CHAPTER 8 • Jesus the Revolutionary

1. The chapter discusses several ideas people have had about Judas Iscariot and his motivation in betraying Jesus. How do you respond to them?

2. Many people dislike it when a preacher discusses political matters from the pulpit. What is your view?

3. Many people think Jesus rejected political revolution. Do you think so? Why or why not?

## CHAPTER 9 • Jesus the Wonderworker

1. What do you think of the miracle of the temple coin in the fish's mouth? How about Jesus cursing the fig tree?

2. Why do you think Jesus often asked people to keep his miracles a secret?

3. What is the difference between "miracle" and "magic"?

4. Have you or someone close to you experienced a miracle?

## CHAPTER 10 • Jesus in Islam

1. This chapter asserts that Muslims worship the same God Christians worship. You know that some Christians disagree, as do some Muslims. What do you think?

2. Although Muhammed is first among the prophets, Jesus is also very important in the Qu'uran. What might this mean for Muslim and Christian life together where you live?

3. What more would you like to learn about Jesus and Mary in Islam?

## CHAPTER 11 • What I Think

1. My journey into Christ begins in childhood and concludes, at the present time, in the silence of contemplative prayer. Where did yours begin? And where do you find Christ now?

2. My most intimate scriptural connection with Jesus at this time is in the prologue to the gospel of John *(In the beginning was the word . . .)*. Where do you find yours?

3. You have noticed that I am not overly concerned with the historicity of the details of Jesus's life and ministry and find their meaning more important than whether or not they are factual. What is your view? Does it trouble you when someone raises doubts about whether or not something in Scripture really happened?